# Homer

# The Essential *Iliad*

D0851788

# Homer

# The Essential *Iliad*

Translated and Edited by
STANLEY LOMBARDO

Introduction by
SHEILA MURNAGHAN

Hackett Publishing Company, Inc.
Indianapolis/Cambridge

Copyright © 2000 by Hackett Publishing Company, Inc.

All rights reserved

Printed in the United States of America

10 09 08 07     3 4 5 6 7

For further information, please address

Hackett Publishing Company, Inc.
P. O. Box 44937
Indianapolis, Indiana 46244–0937

www.hackettpublishing.com

Cover photo: *Into the Jaws of Death*. June 6, 1944
Reproduced by courtesy of the U.S. Coast Guard

Cover design by Abigail Coyle and Brian Rak

Interior design by Meera Dash

An audiobook edition of this title narrated by Stanley Lombardo is available
from Parmenides Publishing. For more information, please go to:
http://www.parmenides.com.

**Library of Congress Cataloging-in-Publication Data**

Homer.
    [Iliad. English. Selections]
    The essential Iliad / Homer ; translated and edited by
Stanley Lombardo ; introduction by Sheila Murnaghan.
      p. cm.
    Abridged edition of the translator's version of Iliad, published in 1997.
    Includes bibliographical references.
    ISBN 0-87220-543-6 — ISBN 0-87220-542-8 (pbk.)
    1. Epic poetry, Greek—Translations into English.   2. Achilles
(Greek mythology)—Poetry.   3. Trojan War—Poetry.   I. Homer.
Iliad. English.   II. Lombardo, Stanley, 1943–   III. Title.

PA4025.A35 L66    2000
883'.01—dc21                                                    00-033421

ISBN-13: 978-0-87220-543-7 (cloth)
ISBN-13: 978-0-87220-542-0 (pbk.)

# Contents

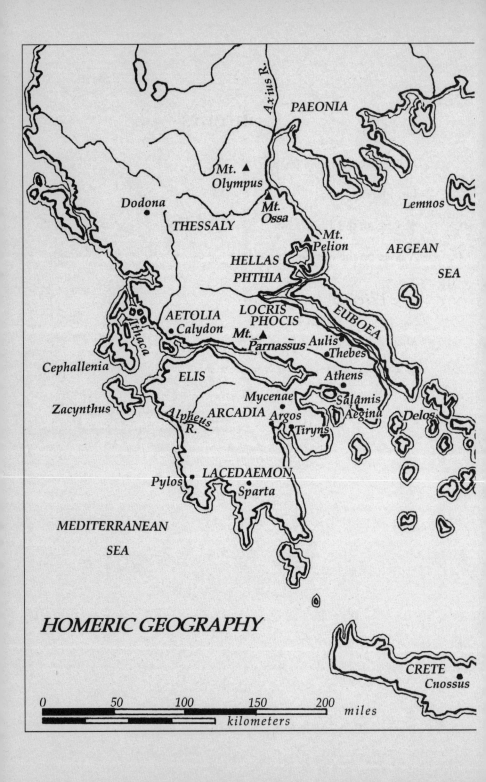

HOMERIC GEOGRAPHY

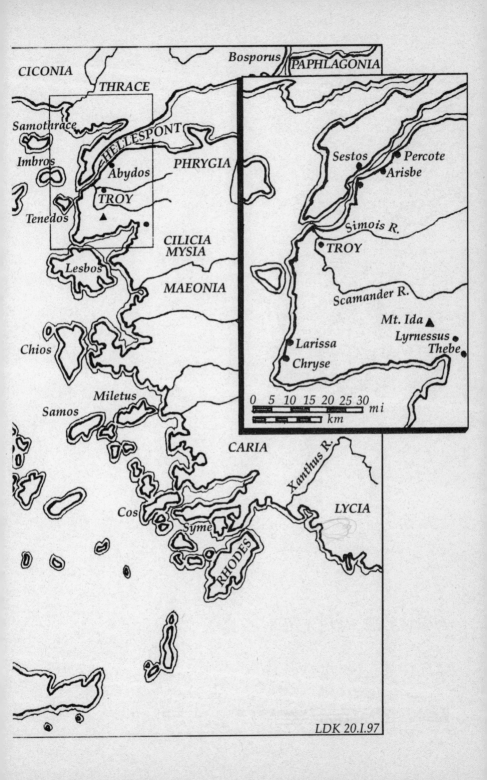

CICONIA

THRACE

Bosporus

PAPHLAGONIA

Samothrace

Imbros

HELLESPONT

Abydos

PHRYGIA

TROY

Tenedos

CILICIA
MYSIA

Lesbos

MAEONIA

Sestos

Percote

Arisbe

Simois R.

TROY

Scamander R.

Mt. Ida

Lyrnessus

Thebe

Larissa

Chryse

0  5  10  15  20  25  30  mi
km

Chios

Miletus

Samos

CARIA

Xanthus R.

Cos

Syme

LYCIA

RHODES

LDK 20.I.97

# Introduction

The *Iliad* is the story of a raging anger and its human toll. The poem recounts "the rage of Achilles," the greatest of the Greek heroes fighting in the war against Troy. Achilles' rage is superhuman (the Greek word translated as "rage," *mēnis*, is used otherwise only of gods) and aligned with cosmic forces: it fulfills the purposes of the supreme god Zeus and brings overwhelming destruction both to Achilles' Greek companions and to their enemies, the Trojans. This rage, the poet tells us,

> . . . cost the Greeks
> Incalculable pain, pitched countless souls
> Of heroes into Hades' dark,
> And left their bodies to rot as feasts
> For dogs and birds, as Zeus' will was done.   (1.2–6)*

And yet this far-reaching fury has its origins, not in the enmity of the Greeks and Trojans, but in the day-to-day tensions of the Greek camp, where a long-standing rivalry between Achilles and his commander Agamemnon flares up in a bitter quarrel. As it opens with this episode of internecine strife, the *Iliad* draws us into a world of warrior aristocrats for whom honor, gained and regained in the front lines of battle, is paramount. Under conditions of extreme pressure, their carefully cultivated distinctions of status give way to contention and hostility.

The story begins with a series of fateful blunders on the part of Agamemnon. Agamemnon has as a war prize a woman, Chryseis, who is the daughter of a priest of the god Apollo. When her father appeals to him to return her, invoking Apollo and offering a rich ransom, Agamemnon rudely dismisses him until Apollo sends a plague against the Greeks, which forces Agamemnon to give Chryseis back. Insisting that his loss of Chryseis must be compensated, Agamemnon

*Line numbers in the Introduction and in the margins of the translation refer to the translation.

decides to take a prize from another leader. He soon fixes on Briseis, the prize of Achilles, whose superiority as a fighter has been a source of friction between them and who has challenged Agamemnon's shaky authority by taking the lead in coping with the plague and by pointing out that the Greeks have no undistributed prizes to replace Chryseis with. For Achilles, Agamemnon's decision means public humiliation and an insulting disregard for his own hard-won status as the best of the Greeks, and he explodes with vicious taunts.

> You bloated drunk,
> With a dog's eyes and a rabbit's heart!
> You've never had the guts to buckle on armor in battle
> Or come out with the best fighting Greeks
> On any campaign! Afraid to look Death in the eye,
> Agamemnon? It's far more profitable
> To hang back in the army's rear—isn't it?—
> Confiscating prizes from any Greek who talks back
> And bleeding your people dry.                    (1.235–44)

Achilles' anger quickly escalates as he follows his fighting words with an aggressive gesture. He slams to the ground the scepter, "studded with gold," that for generations has marked the right to speak in the Greek assembly, invoking its authority for a devastating threat.

> By this scepter, which will never sprout leaf
> Or branch again since it was cut from its stock
> In the mountains, which will bloom no more
> Now that bronze has pared off leaf and bark,
> And which now the sons of the Greeks hold in their hands
> At council, upholding Zeus' laws—
>                              By this scepter I swear:
> When every last Greek desperately misses Achilles,
> Your remorse won't do any good then,
> When Hector the man-killer swats you down like flies.
> And you will eat your heart out
> Because you failed to honor the best Greek of all.
>                                                  (1.248–59)

Achilles' sense of unfair deprivation and his frustration with Agamemnon express themselves in an instinctive response that has far-reaching and unforeseeable consequences, as he turns his back on the whole community of Greeks, whose customs and traditions are embodied in the scepter he throws down, and seeks confirmation of his value in the triumph of their enemy Hector. The rest of the *Iliad* works out these consequences, charting the course of Achilles' rage as it intensifies, changes direction, and finally subsides. Achilles' self-willed estrangement from his former companions places him in unexpected situations that open up new and often painful perspectives on his role as a supremely great warrior. As it tells this story, the *Iliad* offers a full-scale examination of strife as an inescapable feature of human experience. All the characters in the poem must struggle to survive, endure, and make something of value out of conditions of constant conflict, which exist at all levels of the universe: in the clashes of divinities, in the drawn-out war between the Greeks and the Trojans, and in the tensions and rivalries of individuals.

## The *Iliad* and the Trojan Legend

The Trojan legend, in which the quarrel of Achilles and Agamemnon is a brief episode, concerns a central event of Greek mythology. The Greeks (or, in Homer's own term, the Achaeans) band together and cross the Aegean Sea to wage war against Troy, a gracious, prosperous city in Asia Minor (present-day Turkey). Their motive is revenge, for the Trojan prince Paris has stolen Helen, the most beautiful woman in the world, from her husband Menelaus, a major Greek chieftain. Under the leadership of Menelaus' brother Agamemnon, the Greeks fight around Troy for ten years and finally succeed in destroying the city and regaining Helen. The *Iliad* gets its title, which in Greek is *Ilias* and means the story of Troy, from one of the Greek names for Troy, *Ilios* or *Ilion*.

The *Iliad* focuses on Achilles' clash with Agamemnon, which occurs in the final year of the war. But that brief episode is presented in ways that allow it to stand for or suggest the whole of the larger story of which it is part. The events of the *Iliad* represent a decisive turning point in the war. Although Achilles remains stubbornly resistant to Agamemnon's attempts to appease him, he does eventually return to battle, drawn back by an overwhelming need to avenge the death of his closest companion, Patroclus. Patroclus at first joins Achilles in his withdrawal from the war but is eventually overcome by pity for the Greeks. In Achilles' absence, the Greeks are dying in large numbers, and the Trojans, led by Hector, are threatening to burn the Greek ships and so to cut the Greeks off from any hope of returning home, even in disgrace. Patroclus borrows Achilles' armor and returns to battle in Achilles' place. Although he fights brilliantly, killing a major Trojan hero, Sarpedon, he is eventually killed by Hector. Shamed and outraged by Patroclus' death, Achilles is filled with anger against Hector and returns to the battlefield, where he eventually meets and kills Hector.

The *Iliad* ends soon after this, with Achilles' decision to return Hector's body to his father, Priam, and with the funeral for Hector that can then take place. But it is clear that the story of the Trojan war is effectively over: by killing Hector, Achilles has eliminated Troy's indispensable defender, assuring the fall of the city and the victory of the Greeks. The story of Achilles is also over: as he learns from his mother, Thetis, who is a goddess, his own death is fated to follow soon after Hector's. The poet goes out of his way to keep us aware of these looming consequences, although he does not recount them. As they mourn over Hector, the Trojans anticipate the loss of their city and their own defeated future. The death of Achilles is expressed symbolically in the death of Patroclus, who represents for Achilles a kind of second self.

Epic is a monumental form which recounts events with far-reaching historical consequences, sums up the values and achievements of an entire culture, and documents the fullness and variety of the world. While the *Iliad* uses Achilles' story as a means of organizing and concentrating its portrait of the Trojan war, it differs from the sharply focused explorations of individual experience found in many modern novels or in classical tragedy. One of its aims is to record the sheer number of people, each with his or her own history and circumstances, whose lives are decisively shaped by the war, whether by sounding their names in a virtuoso list of the participants such as the Catalogue of Ships (Book 2), or by focusing in on a particular warrior's final moments on the battlefield, or by taking us into Troy, where the women and old men of the city live as anguished spectators of the war. Achilles' story gains in grandeur and significance because of the countless others who are affected by his departure from the war and his eventual return and whose individual efforts his own choices illuminate. His brilliant exploits acquire their meaning in the context of the large-scale cooperative venture of the Greek expedition. The *Iliad* is the portrait of an entire society, structured around the experience of one individual who struggles to define himself within it and against it.

## Heroic Society

The society that the *Iliad* portrays and that Achilles rejects when he slams down the scepter is a distinctive one, an aristocratic, warrior society, centered on battlefield achievement and its rewards. At the top of its hierarchical structure are heroes, superior men who are descendants of gods as well as of mortals. Heroes are born into positions of prominence, which they also reaffirm by their public actions and especially by courageous performance in combat. Their high status is expressed in social gestures (such as how they are addressed); in special privileges (where they sit at a feast); in their share of the tangible wealth of the group (in such forms as wine, meat, tripods, cattle, land, and women); and in the intangible reward of reputation or fame. The communal life of these heroes is highly ceremonious; as they eat together, worship the gods together, participate in councils together, and enter battle together, they follow prescribed forms of speech and behavior that knit them together as a group, that express the honor that they are continually granting and receiving, and that endow their harsh labors with the elegance and orderliness of civilization.

Book 12 of the *Iliad* contains a famous speech that seems to sum up the workings of this social system. It is delivered by Sarpedon, the son of Zeus himself, who is a prominent warrior from an area in Asia Minor called Lycia, fighting on the Trojan side. Here it is important to note that the Trojans and their allies are depicted as having the same values and customs as the Greeks; while the *Iliad* recounts a myth that played a major role in the formation of Greek identity, it does not present the Greeks' enemies as alien. Homeric warfare involves a great deal of talking as well as fighting, and before plunging into battle, Sarpedon turns to his friend Glaucus and offers a kind of meditation on why they willingly accept this experience of violence, chaos, and likely death.

Glaucus, you know how you and I
Have the best of everything in Lycia—

Seats, cuts of meat, full cups, everybody
Looking to us as if we were gods?
Not to mention our estates on the Xanthus,
Fine orchards and riverside wheat fields.
Well, now we have to take our stand at the front,
Where all the best fight, and face the heat of battle,
So that many an armored Lycian will say,
"So they're not inglorious after all,
Our Lycian lords who eat fat sheep
And drink the sweetest wine. No,
They're strong, and fight with our best."
Ah, my friend, if you and I could only
Get out of this war alive and then
Be immortal and ageless all of our days,
I would never again fight among the foremost
Or send you into battle where men win glory.
But, as it is, death is everywhere
In more shapes than we can count,
And since no mortal is immune or can escape,
Let's go forward, either to give glory
To another man, or get glory from him.          (12.320–42)

Sarpedon confidently outlines a series of bargains and calcula-
tions on which his society rests. People like him and Glaucus get
more honor and more material rewards than other people because
they do more, fighting harder than others to further the interests of
the community as a whole and especially fighting in the front lines,
where the risk of death is greatest. They accept this heightened risk
because of those rewards and because death is inescapable. Since life
is finite, they are willing for it to be cut short if they can enjoy honor
and privileges while it lasts and if they can win some permanent fame
that will outlive them. Part of what makes heroic combat so breath-
taking is this head-on response to mortality. Instead of evading
death, heroes make it their own, inflicting it on others and courting
it for themselves.

As Sarpedon describes it, this system works smoothly, and he
does indeed follow his speech by entering the battle (although his
cheerful acceptance comes to seem more poignant in retrospect
when he is killed by Patroclus). But the *Iliad* does not just describe
this society and celebrate the achievements of its leaders; it also

reveals its flaws and weaknesses as they emerge under conditions of severe strain. The *Iliad* is set at a time when the war has been going on for so long that both sides have been drained of resources and everyone involved is exhausted. Even if it can survive, Troy has lost the wealth and manpower that made it a great city. The Greeks have been cut off for nine years from the rich fields and glorious feasts that supposedly make combat worthwhile. Both sides have trouble remembering why they are fighting in the first place.

Under these conditions, calculations like Sarpedon's break down, and the point of a warrior ethic of honor and courage is increasingly open to question. The crisis in the Greek camp, with which the plot begins, reflects the particular strains that arise when a group of heroes, who are all preeminent at home, as Sarpedon is in Lycia, have to temper their individual claims in order to work together as a unified force. This situation is further complicated by the intervention of the gods through Apollo's plague. The forced return of Chryseis disrupts the harmony achieved by the acceptable distribution of booty. With one fewer prize to go around, it is no longer possible for every hero to feel appropriately honored, and there is nothing to keep the competition between Agamemnon and Achilles from flaring up in open hostility.

The desperate reactions of both heroes to the threat of losing a prize show how fully their sense of self is bound up in these external marks of honor. They know themselves in large part through their social status, which is created and expressed in public settings. Furthermore, as Sarpedon's speech makes clear, these prizes acquire added value from their supremely high price: the heroes' willingness to risk their lives every time they enter battle. The conflict between Achilles and Agamemnon also shows how hard it can be to apportion honor in a way that satisfies everyone. Agamemnon's implicit decision that if there is only one prize, it should go to him, not to Achilles, raises stubborn questions about the relative value of a great fighter and a king, questions which have clearly been causing tension in the Greek camp for some time, and which Achilles throws in Agamemnon's face when he calls him a coward and labels himself "the best Greek of all." In contrast to Sarpedon's entrance into battle, Achilles' repudiation of Agamemnon's leadership expresses a loss of confidence in the ability of his community to reward his efforts. He then launches an attempt to find adequate compensation outside the conventional words and actions of that community and, in doing so, forces every reader of the *Iliad* to consider how and whether this is possible.

## The Homeric Gods

Achilles' withdrawal from the Greek camp is fueled by his strong sense of difference from its other members, which is manifested in his superior fighting ability and also in his birth: he has a divine mother, Thetis, a widely powerful sea goddess, as well as a mortal father, Peleus. Through Thetis he is able to appeal to Zeus, the king of the gods and the commanding figure of the universe. Zeus honors his appeal by making the Trojans succeed in the war, so that Agamemnon and the other Greeks become agonizingly aware of what Achilles' alienation is costing them.

In turning to Zeus, Achilles turns to a realm of powerful beings who are constantly involved in human affairs and who resemble human beings but who also differ from them in important ways. The Homeric gods can control all the different forces that shape human life, from the weather to emotions to social practices and institutions. The distinctness of these forces and their potential for conflict is expressed in the existence of a range of individual gods with different associations: for example, Poseidon is the god of the sea, Aphrodite of erotic love, Athena of craftsmanship and of war as an instrument of justice, Ares of war in its violence and brutality, Apollo of music and prophecy, and so on. At the same time, the gods are linked as members of a single family, under the authority of its head, Zeus, whose supremacy is expressed in his control of the sky and his possession of thunder and lightning as weapons.

Because of their superior power, the gods can command the obedience and veneration of human beings, who must seek their favor through offerings, most often the sacrifice of animals, and they are constantly able to intervene in human life. In fact, all human endeavors occur under the sponsorship of the gods, and Homeric poetry frequently alludes to the divine support that underlies one human act after another. On the battlefield, a spear often meets its mark because a god makes sure that it does or falls uselessly to the ground because a god has chosen to deflect it. The gods have individual favorites whose interests they promote, and they also take sides in the war. Thus Aphrodite is on the Trojan side, and Hera,

Zeus' wife, and Athena, his daughter, are on the Greek side, because of an event that lies behind the story of the *Iliad*, although it is mentioned only once, toward the end of the poem, the so-called Judgment of Paris. Paris' theft of Helen—the occasion of the Trojan War—has been carried out with the help of Aphrodite as a reward for picking her over Hera and Athena in a beauty contest. As this episode reveals, the gods' superior power does not make them nobler than mortals, or less passionate in the pursuit of their individual interests.

Not only do the Homeric gods have more power than human beings, they also have greater knowledge, in particular of fate; they know what is destined to happen and act consciously to bring that about. For many modern readers, the activities of the gods and the existence of fate seem to drain the human characters of their autonomy, to turn them into puppets. It is important to recognize, however, that divine intervention is almost always in harmony with the preexisting qualities and instincts of those human characters. Divine favor may make possible displays of heroic excellence, but it is also a response to that excellence; in an unbreakably circular logic, men are heroic because the gods help them, and the gods help them because they are heroic. When gods influence events, they work through impulses that are already present in the characters, and the poet often presents events as doubly motivated, stemming both from the plans and projects of the gods and from those of the human characters.

The confluence of divine intervention and human impulse can be illustrated from an episode early in the poem. Just before Achilles insults Agamemnon and slams down the scepter, he almost kills him instead. As he reaches for his sword, he wavers:

> . . . should he
> Draw the sharp sword that hung by his thigh,
> Scatter the ranks and gut Agamemnon,
> Or control his temper, repress his rage?  (1.199–202)

At this point, Athena comes down, grabs him by the hair, and tells him not to kill Agamemnon, promising that he will get many more prizes in the end if he restrains himself. A modern reader may want to interpret Athena here as symbolizing a psychological force within

Achilles, an intrinsic capacity for restraint and rational calculation. Granting her the external reality she has for Homer, we can still see that her intervention makes Achilles decide on a course of action he was already considering.

Similarly, fate does not function in the Homeric world as a force that causes characters to do what they otherwise would not. Human beings bring about what is fated through all of the individual, often short-sighted decisions they make while pursuing their various goals. Knowledge of fate, which the gods possess and occasionally share with mortals, is like advance knowledge of the plot of a novel or a film. It allows a greater appreciation of the direction of events that for most characters seem random and open-ended, but it does not alter the behavior of those characters. Certainly the human characters in the *Iliad* experience their lives as involving choices, often difficult ones, and they expect to be judged by the consequences of their choices despite the fact that those choices—like all human actions—are sponsored by the gods and bring about what is fated.

While the Homeric gods resemble humans to a striking extent in their appearance and their emotions, they differ in the crucial respect that they are not subject to permanent change, including above all death; they are immortal. This makes them profoundly different from mortals in their values and their behaviors, because they do not—and cannot—share the attachments and commitments that humans make in the face of death. This difference is pointedly illustrated early in the *Iliad*, when the conflict in the Greek camp with which the poem begins is followed by an episode of conflict among the gods. When Thetis comes to Zeus and asks him to help Achilles by making the Trojans do well in the war, so Agamemnon will recognize his mistake and restore Achilles' honor, Hera suspects what is going on and, because she herself favors the Greeks, becomes angry. When Zeus returns to the divine circle, she berates him, and the gods' habitual gaiety is threatened by discord.

But while the discord among the Greeks continues for many days and does not end until many men, both Trojan and Greek, have been killed, this divine quarrel is instantly patched up, as Hera's son Hephaestus persuades her to give up her anger. He tells her a story to remind her that there is no point resisting Zeus, who is more powerful than the rest of them, and he reminds her that a quarrel between her and Zeus will spoil the gods' fun:

This is terrible; it's going to ruin us all.
If you two quarrel like this over mortals
It's bound to affect us gods. There'll be no more
Pleasure in our feasts if we let things turn ugly.     (1.606–9)

This episode brings out two key differences between divine and human society. Among the gods there is a clear hierarchy: Zeus may have had struggles in the past, and he may continue to suffer challenges, but he is the strongest god and always will be, so there is no lasting good to be gained by resisting him. Among the human characters, the power structure is less clear and more subject to change, so that Achilles does have reason to contest Agamemnon's authority. And the gods, having nothing to lose, see no point in fighting over what they care about. Hera would rather that the Greeks not do badly in the war, but their losses do not mean enough to her that she would sacrifice the pleasure of a feast because of them. Achilles, on the other hand, goes to great lengths to protest his loss of Briseis, because she represents the honor which is his only compensation for the likely loss of his life.

Only in a few rare instances are the gods shown as suffering the constraints that define human life, and those involve cases where they are bound to humans by the tie of parenthood. In a surprising episode in Book 16, Zeus himself experiences the demands of fate, with its intimate connection to human mortality, as a painful limitation. As the moment approaches when his own son Sarpedon is fated to die at the hands of Patroclus, Zeus toys with the idea of reversing fate but backs off, weeping tears of blood, when the other gods make it clear that they will not support him. Much more extensively, the *Iliad* portrays Achilles' mother, Thetis, as deeply pained by the fate of her son, whose present sufferings and future death she constantly mourns.

Despite the sympathy of his mother, when Achilles turns away from his fellow humans to Zeus in his quest for satisfaction, he is relying on a being who not only is vastly more powerful than they but also has his own distinct purposes and values. While Achilles imagines at that point that Zeus' only intention is to restore Achilles' lost honor, Zeus' role in the events of the *Iliad* is, in fact, much more complicated and enigmatic. The aims of the human characters and the other gods, through whom Zeus works, are relatively clear, but the "will of Zeus" itself remains opaque. Although he is the ulti-

mate source of most good things in human life, and he reacts with
distaste to Hera's intransigent hatred of the Trojans, he seems mys-
teriously bent on the perpetuation of the war to the point of maxi-
mum destruction. As Achilles later concludes, renouncing his rage
against Agamemnon and wondering at its origins: "Somehow it has
pleased Zeus / That many Greeks should die" (19.291–2; not in this
volume).

## Achilles

With Zeus' help, Achilles is able to bring Agamemnon to his knees.
The Trojans are so successful that they push the Greeks back into
their ships, around which the Greeks have built a defensive wall and
ditch; the Trojans now camp on the plain, no longer retreating into
Troy at night. Recognizing that their cause is lost without Achilles,
Agamemnon sends three ambassadors to him with an offer of
amends that includes the return of Briseis and a huge number of
additional prizes. In a stunning response that overturns all expecta-
tions, Achilles rejects this offer. In a long and passionate speech, he
announces that he is going to leave Troy and return home. While
the force of this speech is unmistakable, its exact meaning has been
much debated: making sense of this difficult speech is a major chal-
lenge for readers of the *Iliad*.

    This speech is so challenging because Achilles' continued sense
of outrage expresses itself in contradictory positions, and he shifts
back and forth between them. In part he is simply still furious at
what Agamemnon has done, unable to forget Agamemnon's errors
and his own mistreatment:

> He cheated me, wronged me. Never again.
> He's had it. He can go to hell in peace,
> The half-wit that Zeus has made him.
> His gifts? His gifts mean nothing to me.     (9.386–9)

But Achilles' loss of respect for Agamemnon, the source of the gifts
through which he has experienced his own value, sparks a much
more fundamental questioning of the value of those gifts themselves,
gifts that for someone like Achilles, who already has plenty of pos-
sessions, have no meaning outside their ability to confer honor. As a

result, Achilles' expressions of ongoing anger are set side by side with radical reconsiderations of the basic principles of heroic culture, such as the assumption that honor-bearing gifts are a worthwhile compensation for the loss of life in battle.

> Nothing is worth my life, not all the riches
> They say Troy held before the Greeks came,
> Not all the wealth in Phoebus Apollo's
> Marble shrine up in craggy Pytho.
> Cattle and flocks are there for the taking;
> You can always get tripods and chestnut horses.
> But a man's life cannot be won back
> Once his breath has passed beyond his clenched teeth.    (9.415–22)

He asks as well whether a courageous death in the front lines of battle really is meaningfully different from and better than any other death.

> It doesn't matter if you stay in camp or fight—
> In the end, everybody comes out the same.
> Coward and hero get the same reward:
> You die whether you slack off or work.             (9.324–7)

As when he slams down the scepter in his first impulse to quit the Greek cause, Achilles expresses simultaneously a deep attachment to the system that he has trusted in and that has betrayed him and a new detachment born from that betrayal, now elaborated into a full-scale critique of heroic values. In his continuing frustration, he asks a great deal of his culture, perhaps more than it can give. He tells the ambassadors that he will not yield until Agamemnon has "paid in full for all my grief" (9.400), holding out for a complete restitution that may not be possible. Agamemnon has certainly erred in the past, and he may be erring still in approaching Achilles through ambassadors rather than apologizing in person, but the gifts he offers are, as the wise veteran Nestor puts it, "beyond reproach" (9.168; not in this volume), and he cannot undo the past or stop being king. Even as he insists on these demands, Achilles also voices a new and unparalleled clarity about how little his culture has to offer, about the paltriness of the gifts and privileges with which men honor each other compared to the immensity of death.

Here too, Achilles' independence from the other Greeks and from the values that animate them is supported by his special closeness to the gods. In his speech, he brings up the privileged information that he has from his divine mother.

> My mother Thetis, a moving silver grace,
> Tells me two fates sweep me on to my death.
> If I stay here and fight, I'll never return home,
> But my glory will be undying forever.
> If I return home to my dear fatherland
> My glory is lost but my life will be long,
> And death that ends all will not catch me soon.   (9.423–9)

Through his special access to divine foreknowledge, Achilles knows that if he fights in the war he certainly will die. This certainty sets him off from other heroes, who can always hope, against all odds, to be spared, and it gives him a sense of freedom and choice, an ability to choose against the unequal bargain of life for honor that more ordinary warriors regularly enter into.

Achilles' newfound clarity about the inadequacy of the system in which he and the other Greeks have operated brings a new perspective to the poem, allowing it to show how the heroic world may look from a position outside it. But, as with all human vision, Achilles' clarity is only partial and is accompanied by blindness. Some of what Achilles cannot see is expressed in the speeches of the ambassadors who respond to him. Horrified by Achilles' decision, which spells certain disaster for all of them, they offer answers to his complaints that are deeply embedded in their common heritage. First Phoenix, Achilles' beloved old tutor, tells him "a very old story" (9.542) about another hero, Meleager, who like Achilles becomes angry at his community and withdraws from it during a war. Like Achilles, Meleager is offered rich gifts if he will return and is solicited by his friends and family, but he remains adamant until the moment when his city is about to be destroyed and his wife, Cleopatra, begs him to save it. Meleager returns to battle and saves his city, but at that point the gifts are no longer available. Phoenix's story responds to Achilles' claim that gifts are not adequate compensation for fighting, by showing that there are other reasons why people fight besides honor. If you are going to end up fighting anyway, he points out, you might as well take the gifts when they are offered.

Ajax in his response draws, not on a traditional story, but on a shared institution, that of the blood price. He bitterly criticizes Achilles for his savage heart and lack of pity for the Greeks, who have loved and honored him, and he counters Achilles' sense of outraged superiority with another model of human behavior, one that involves self-restraint and acceptance of loss.

> A man accepts compensation
> For a murdered brother, a dead son.
> The killer goes on living in the same town
> After paying blood money, and the bereaved
> Restrains his proud spirit and broken heart
> Because he has received payment.      (9.652–7)

While Achilles rejects Agamemnon's gifts because they do not seem adequate compensation for the loss of honor he has suffered or the loss of life he faces, Ajax points out that people regularly do accept inadequate recompense for the most wrenching losses. Faced with a loss that can never be made up, they let go of their attachment to the dead and are content with the only compensation there is.

These speeches answer Achilles' concerns obliquely, and his own response to them is ambiguous. In his words, he repeats both his undiminished anger at Agamemnon, telling Ajax that

> Everything you say is after my own heart.
> But I swell with rage when I think of how
> The son of Atreus treated me like dirt.      (9.668–70)

and his sense of transcendent detachment from the Greeks, telling Phoenix that "I don't need that kind of honor. . . . My honor comes from Zeus" (9.624–5). But he does keep retreating from his announced plan of leaving Troy, first telling Phoenix that he will decide in the morning whether or not to go and then telling Ajax that he will stay out of the war until he is personally threatened, until Hector is about to burn his own huts and ships. The episode concludes with a disparity between what Achilles is able to think and say and what he is actually able to do that the rest of the poem must resolve.

The debate between Achilles and Agamemnon's ambassadors ends there and is never explicitly taken up again, but the rest of the

*Iliad* tells how Achilles ends up doing what he has so adamantly insisted he will not do, fighting again for the Greeks. And, in doing so, Achilles reenacts the pattern set by Phoenix's story of Meleager: Achilles too returns to battle to save his community through the agency of the person he cares most about, in his case Patroclus (whose name inverts and echoes the name of Meleager's wife, Cleopatra).

The relationship between Achilles and Patroclus involves both intense closeness (they are so close that later Greeks who idealized male homosexual relations assumed they were lovers, although there is no indication of that in the *Iliad*) and a stark contrast: while Achilles is violent, quick to anger, and jealous of his own honor, Patroclus is gentle, concerned for the bonds of friendship between members of the army, and compassionate, and he reenters the war out of pity for the many Greeks who are dying because of Achilles' absence. When he rejoins the battle, Patroclus does so as Achilles' surrogate, literally impersonating him by wearing his armor, and he represents Achilles' double as well as his opposite. Patroclus becomes consumed with the kind of rage for combat associated with Achilles, and he fights with risky brilliance, achieving glorious success by killing Sarpedon but also exposing himself to death at the hands of Hector. Conversely, Patroclus' death awakens in Achilles a sense of connectedness to other people as he experiences anguish for the loss of his beloved friend and shame for his failure to protect him. Shaken from his sense of glorious superiority, Achilles now sees himself, in his willed isolation, as worthless, "a dead weight on the earth," as he tells his mother (18.109).

For Achilles, Patroclus' death is a shattering reminder of those other reasons for fighting that he seemed to forget in his obsession with Agamemnon's faults and the insufficiency of honor. In their self-presentation and their rational calculations, heroes may stress the material rewards and status that come from fighting, as Sarpedon does in his speech to Glaucus, but they are also inspired by concern for the communities they protect and by deep bonds between each other: although Sarpedon may present their situation as a set of bargains, he does also address Glaucus as "my friend."

This is not to say, however, that Achilles in returning to battle is also returning to the Greek warrior community, with all of its rituals and customs. The rage that he has felt toward Agamemnon is now supplanted by a new rage against Hector, and he fights with a viciousness and single-mindedness that contrast sharply with the rest of the fighting described in the *Iliad*. That fighting, while brutal, is nonetheless balanced by civilized practices like pausing to eat, to sleep, or to bury the dead. As he seeks revenge for Patroclus' death, Achilles seems more like an elemental force than an ordinary warrior (in his indiscriminate violence, taking on even the river Scamander), and he stands outside the normal practices of human warfare. As he rejoins the Greek army, he has no patience for stopping to let the men eat and drink or even for receiving the gifts that Agamemnon has promised him; and Odysseus, who is much more finely attuned to the protocols of heroic society, has to insist that he go through those motions. Meeting for the second time a Trojan warrior, Lycaon, whom before he has been willing to take captive and hold for ransom rather than kill, Achilles is now unmoved by Lycaon's pleas, and, with a single cut to the collarbone, he buries his sword in Lycaon's chest.

Achilles' distance from the normal decorum of warfare is most pointed and explicit at the moment when he finally encounters the object of his fury, Hector. Hector proposes a bargain whereby the winner of their combat will return the loser's body to his family for the loving and ceremonious burial with which people attempt to cure the insult of violent death, but Achilles has no interest in that:

> Don't try to cut any deals with me, Hector.
> Do lions make peace treaties with men?
> Do wolves and lambs agree to get along?
> No, they hate each other to the core,
> And that's how it is between you and me.
> No talk of agreements until one of us
> Falls and gluts Ares with his blood.    (22.287–93)

Although he is motivated to fight by his love for Patroclus, Achilles remains isolated from all other members of the human community, rightly comparing himself to the most savage animals. Still set apart by his godlike knowledge of fate—made all the clearer by Thetis when she tells him, as he decides to return, that he will die next after Hector: "Hector's death means yours" (18.101)—Achilles fights unhampered by any hope of survival, with nothing to lose.

# Hector

In rejecting Hector's proposal, Achilles distances himself from a
hero who, unlike Achilles, has always remained identified with the
values and rituals of his society. Throughout the *Iliad*, Hector and
the other Trojans provide a different perspective on heroism from
the Greeks, as they fight around and for their own city, battling for
the survival of their homes and families, rather than for the glory to
be won in a foreign expedition. While Hector shares the courage
and fighting ability typified by Achilles, he also manifests the con-
nection to his community associated with Patroclus, and, as he too
struggles with his identity as a hero, he does so in the context of his
relations with family members rather than with his commander.

Earlier in the poem, Hector, like Achilles, has been faced with
a choice, although it is formulated differently and he gives a very dif-
ferent response. A large part of Book 6 of the *Iliad* is devoted to an
episode in which Hector returns from the battlefield to Troy, the
shared space of his community, and meets there a series of women:
his mother, Hecuba; his sister-in-law, Helen; and his wife, Androma-
che. What emerges from these encounters is how fully, as a warrior,
Hector is cut off from the community he is risking his life to protect.
His mother offers him some wine and invites him to pour a libation
to Zeus, but he points out that he is unfit for this routine religious
observance:

> I have too much reverence to pour a libation
> With unwashed hands to Zeus almighty,
> Or to pray to Cronion in the black cloudbanks
> Spattered with blood and the filth of battle.     (6.277–80)

Andromache has their young child, Astyanax, with her, and Hector's
cherished son is terrified by his father's war helmet and shrinks from
him until Hector takes it off and puts it on the ground. The possibil-
ity of lingering in the city with these women is presented as a dan-
gerous temptation, as Hector expresses fear that Hecuba's wine will
rob him of his strength and fends off Helen's seductive invitation to
sit down beside her.

The most compelling temptation is presented by Andromache,
who wretchedly points out that Hector's courage is bound to bring
his death and with it the destruction of the city he is supposed to be

saving. Dwelling in painful detail on the bitter life of enslavement and humiliation that lies ahead for her and Astyanax, she asks him to give up his commitment to fighting aggressively in the front lines, suggesting that he fall back to the wall and fight defensively. Hector expresses sympathy for her position and anguish over her fate and his, but is unable to do as she asks:

> Yes, Andromache, I worry about all this myself,
> But my shame before the Trojans and their wives,
> With their long robes trailing, would be too terrible
> If I hung back from battle like a coward.
> And my heart won't let me. I have learned to be
> One of the best, to fight in Troy's first ranks,
> Defending my father's honor and my own. (6.463–69)

Like Achilles when he rejects Agamemnon's ambassadors, Hector is sacrificing his community to his pursuit of honor, but he does so by embracing rather than by rejecting its values, and here the poem reveals a contradiction within heroic values that is in some ways more devastating than Achilles' explicit critique. Hector's words show that his own society has made him unable to respond to his wife's desperate plea, no matter how much he feels for her: his combative instincts are instilled by his training and the social pressures that control his behavior through honor and its opposite, shame. The child Astyanax creates a moment of harmony between Hector and Andromache, as they laugh together at his fear of the helmet, but Hector soon leaves with a prayer that his son may become—like him—a powerful and dedicated warrior.

When Hector finally faces Achilles, he does so as someone who has always stayed within the framework of heroic values and who embodies the blindness and self-destructiveness that are bound up with heroic glory. Buoyed up by his temporary success, Hector has recklessly ignored the good advice of his brother Polydamas and has dismissed an omen from the gods. But, when he first sees Achilles in all his force and passion, Hector's first instinct is to run. Achilles chases him three times around the city, until Athena disguises herself as Hector's brother Deïphobus and tricks him into stopping and facing Achilles by promising to support him. Hector does face Achilles, but, when he loses his spear and turns—he thinks—to Deïphobus for another, he finds no one there. Realizing at once that he is alone and doomed, he continues to fight, voicing the essential heroic determination to make something out of inevitable death: ". . . I will not perish without some great deed / That future generations will remember" (22.332–3).

## The Enduring Heart

By killing Hector, Achilles saves the Greeks, opening the way for the taking of Troy and making it possible for them to return home at last. He also secures his own future fame, performing a deed that will be remembered and sung about forever. Having chosen, in the end, a short life, he achieves the glory that goes with it, fighting with a godlike brilliance and a bestial ferocity. With his death now imminent, his story is essentially over. But the *Iliad* does not end here: Achilles does not meet his mortal end without also rediscovering his identity as a mortal; he does not die without first recovering his connection to other human beings.

True to his word, Achilles does not honor Hector's request to return his body to his family. Instead he repeatedly yokes it to his chariot and drags it in the dust around Patroclus' tomb. This vengeful assault on the body of Patroclus' killer is the ultimate expression of Achilles' rage. That rage finally comes to an end when Hector's father, Priam, persuades him to give the body back, after all, in exchange for a rich ransom.

Like all the other events of the *Iliad*, the ransoming of Hector's body stems from both divine and human motives, beginning with the decision on Olympus that Achilles must give the body back. Although the gods are repelled by Achilles' savage behavior, they do not simply take the body away from him but, as always, work through the emotions and practices of human life. Thus Zeus summons Thetis to Olympus, and, on his instructions, she goes down to Achilles and tells him that he must accept Priam's ransom. This action inverts the opening sequence of the poem, in which Thetis goes up to Zeus to get him to do what Achilles wants, and it underscores what the plot of the poem has already revealed, the limits to Achilles' special favor from Zeus.

Achilles' sense of Zeus' favor, his feeling of having honor from Zeus, has allowed him to do what no other hero can, to step outside his warrior culture and voice a detached and godlike perspective on that culture. But Achilles' detachment has a high price, in the lost lives of the many Greeks and Trojans who die while he stays out of the war, and it does not, in the end, protect him from either the danger or the grief of a warrior's life. He experiences the ambiguity of Zeus' favor most bitterly with Patroclus' death, in his stunned realization that he has gotten what he asked for, recognition from the Greeks through Trojan success, but at an intolerable cost that he never envisioned. In his dealings with Zeus, Achilles confronts the painful lessons—the gap between what humans can imagine and long for and what they can actually have, the difficulty of learning except too late and by suffering—that were later to be explored in classical tragedy, and he has experiences that we have come to label "tragic." Like many later tragic characters and like many of the heroes of the *Iliad*, most notably Hector before his death, Achilles performs his most memorable and most valued actions when he feels the gods have abandoned him.

After Thetis' communication, Achilles' return of Hector's body is renegotiated on the human level as Priam makes his dangerous journey into the enemy camp and pleads with Achilles to give up his son's remains. In responding to Priam's plea, Achilles displays and affirms a form of human achievement that is far removed from the energetic initiatives of the battlefield: the patient endurance of suffering. This is the quality that Ajax speaks of in Book 9, when Achilles is unready to hear him, and Ajax's sentiments are recalled in Book 24 by Apollo as he and the other gods condemn Achilles' mistreatment of Hector's body.

> A man may lose someone dearer than Achilles has,
> A brother from the same womb, or a son,
> But when he has wept and mourned, he lets go.
> The Fates have given men an enduring heart.
> (24.50–3; not in this volume)

As Apollo's words make clear, the enduring heart is a peculiarly human virtue, a response to the suffering that human beings experience and gods do not. It is a harsh virtue, in that it demands a certain hard-heartedness, a willingness to let go of the most precious attachments, but it is, after all, an adaptation to harsh conditions. And that eventual letting go makes possible the consolations that human beings are able to find in the face of suffering. In that sense it is, as Apollo describes it, a gift from the gods.

In the final episode of the *Iliad*, both Priam and Achilles command our admiration for their extraordinary endurance, and, as a result, they are each able to gain something of value from even the doomed and heartbreaking situations in which they find themselves. As he makes his appeal to Achilles, kneeling before him as a suppliant and asking him to think of his own father, Peleus, Priam has to give up his hatred of Achilles as the killer of Hector, and he speaks of his action in a way that shows how endurance can be itself a form of heroism:

> I have borne what no man
> Who has walked this earth has ever yet borne.
> I have kissed the hand of the man who killed my son.   (24.541–3)

Doing so, he gains Achilles' awed respect ("You have a heart of iron," 24.560) and the release of his son's body.

To return the body and accept the ransom, Achilles has to let go of his overwhelming attachment to Patroclus, to stop feeling the bitter outrage that has kept him uselessly punishing Hector even after he is dead, but he is able to experience the solace of shared grief as he and Priam mourn together. He is able then to move beyond grief as they eat and drink together and, for a moment, gaze with admiring delight at one another. That Achilles is now able to grant Priam's one desire shows how endurance is a humane as well as a harsh virtue, linked, as Ajax suggests, to pity. Achilles' detachment from the dead Patroclus, for whom he can now do nothing more, allows him to do something meaningful for Priam, who, while his enemy, is still living and can benefit from his action.

As he opens himself up to pity for Priam, Achilles finally comes to terms with his identity as a mortal, bound to other mortals by the common experience of incurable loss. He voices a sense of what it means to be mortal, in an account of Zeus and his role in shaping mortal life that is very different from his earlier vision of Zeus as his particular supporter. He tells Priam that Zeus gives every man gifts from two jars, one of good things, one of evils. To some he gives all evils, to some a mixture a good and evil; to no one does he give all good. To exemplify the life of good mixed with evil that is the best one can hope for, he develops the comparison between Priam and Peleus, to which Priam has appealed. Both are men who have known great prosperity, but have had their lives darkened by the loss of a beloved son. These examples draw our attention to war in particular as a source of human misery. It is through war that mortality is made even more painful than it has to be, as young men die deaths that are early and violent, and parents must bury their children.

In honoring Priam's appeal to remember Peleus, Achilles finally resolves the issue of his mixed parentage. He becomes identified with his mortal father rather than with the divine mother who once made him feel different and freer than other mortals. As he recognizes that Thetis can no longer help him, he no longer shares his sorrows with her, but with another mortal who, even though he is an enemy, meets him on common ground. And by agreeing to accept Priam's ransom, he also resolves the issue of the insufficiency of material rewards that has haunted the entire *Iliad*.

This issue emerges at the very beginning of the poem with Agamemnon, who sets the plot in motion when he refuses to take ransom from the old priest Chryses for his daughter Chryseis; with Priam's successful ransoming of Hector's body, the end of the poem recalls and corrects its beginning. Agamemnon refuses the ransom offered him by Chryses because it does not seem to him adequate to the value he places on Chryseis, who is to him not just an exchangeable sign of honor but a woman he cares for. As we have seen, the same issue comes up with far more urgency in Achilles' rejection of the embassy, when he refuses Agamemnon's gifts because they are not commensurate with the value of his only life. When Achilles takes Priam's ransom, he finally gives up the stubborn insistence on equal compensation that has caused both him and Agamemnon so much grief; he accepts and values that ransom as the only compensation there is.

Both Agamemnon and Achilles show how characteristic it is of human beings to long for and fantasize about complete restitution for whatever they have lost. But that fantasy is ruled out by the very nature of mortal life, in which gifts come from other human beings who are always, like Agamemnon, flawed and in which time is irreversible, choices are finite, and death is incurable. There is in the end no better way than to take whatever meager recompense is offered.

At the same time, the *Iliad* reveals and celebrates the value that people can give to mere material objects, as they embellish their clothes and their armor, as they strip a stick of its leaves, stud it with gold, and turn it into a symbol of communal order, or as they consent to equate robes, cauldrons, and tripods with the life of a beloved friend.

At the end of the *Iliad*, Achilles is in an extraordinary situation, having asserted his superiority to all other living heroes and having secured immortal glory, but not yet dead. Yet he has no more meaningful way of experiencing his greatness than by accepting the ordinary, limited consolations of everyday human life, finding fellowship in the company of others, taking gifts and the honor they convey, eating food, making love, and going to sleep. Nothing brings this home more clearly than the final image of Achilles with which the poem leaves us—asleep in his shelter, with Briseis at his side.

## The Historical Context

We know much less than we would like to about how and when the *Iliad* came into being. Ancient tradition attributed the poem to Homer, who was also considered responsible for another epic about the Trojan legend, the *Odyssey*, which tells about the return of the Greeks from Troy, and several shorter poems about the gods; but we have no reliable information about Homer that can contribute to an understanding of these works.

Where questions of chronology are concerned, it is not really possible to pin the poem to a single historical period. There is a strong—but far from complete—scholarly consensus that the *Iliad* was first written down in something like the form in which we now have it in the last half of the eighth century B.C.E., the time at which the Greeks acquired the art of alphabetic writing and written literature thus became possible. At the same time, we know the *Iliad* to be the result of a long tradition of earlier poetry, stretching back over many centuries, to which we have no direct access, because it was never written down, and which we can approach only through the traces it has left on the *Iliad* and other early Greek literature. The immense scholarly effort devoted to Homeric poetry over the last several centuries has made it clear that the *Iliad* reflects several historical periods, in a complicated amalgam whose layers we can only approximately distinguish.

First, it is important to recognize that the *Iliad* is itself a work of history, that it presents its story as a recollection of long-past events taking place in a time very different from that in which those events are being recalled. The characters in the story are seen as belonging to a superior, even semidivine breed that no longer exists, and they perform actions that no living person could duplicate. This sense of a gap between the world of the poem and the poet and his audience surfaces in occasional comments, as when the poet describes how Diomedes in the middle of combat "Levered up in one hand a slab of stone / Much too large for two men to lift— / As men are now . . ." (5.328–30; not in this volume). It also informs the poem's frequent use of similes, which assimilate the distant world of heroic combat to a more ordinary, everyday world familiar to the poem's audience.

The Trojan legend is a story of large-scale destruction. It includes not only the annihilation of Troy, but the many disruptions, almost as devastating as what they have inflicted on the Trojans, experienced by the Greeks as they return: they are blown off course and lost at sea, or they make it back, only to find their homes in turmoil and their own positions there under attack. For the ancient Greeks, this legend recorded the passing of an age of heroes that was understood to precede the drearier world of the present. To a modern historian, it reflects the end of the first stage of ancient Greek history, which is known as the Bronze Age, after the widespread use of bronze during that time, or the Mycenaean period, after the city of Mycenae, one of the main power centers of that era.

Mycenaean civilization developed in the centuries after 2000 B.C.E., which is approximately when Greek-speaking people first arrived in the area at the southern end of the Balkan peninsula that we now know as Greece. Those Greek-speakers gradually established there a rich civilization dominated by a few powerful cities built around large, highly organized palaces. These palaces were at once fortified military strongholds and centers for international trade, in particular trade with the many islands located in the Aegean Sea, to the east of the Greek mainland. On the largest of those islands, the island of Crete, there was already flourishing, by the time the Mycenaeans arrived in Greece, the rich and sophisticated Minoan civilization, by which the Mycenaeans were heavily influenced and which they came ultimately to dominate.

From the Minoans the Mycenaeans gained, along with many other crafts and institutions, a system of writing: a syllabary, in which each symbol stands for a particular syllable, as opposed to an alphabet—like the Roman alphabet now used to write English—in which each symbol stands for a particular sound. The Mycenaeans adapted the syllabary which the Minoans used to write their own language (a language which, although we have examples of their writing, still has not been deciphered) and used it to write Greek. This earliest Greek writing system is known to present-day scholars as Linear B, and archaeologists excavating at the mainland centers of Mycenae and Pylos have recovered examples of it incised on clay tablets. These tablets contain not—as was hoped when they were found—political treaties, mythological poems, or accounts of religious rituals, but detailed accounts of a highly bureaucratic palace economy: inventories of grain or livestock and lists of palace functionaries assigned to perform such specialized roles as "unguent boiler," "chair-maker," or "bath-pourer."

Mycenaean civilization reached its height at about 1600 B.C.E. and was essentially destroyed in a series of natural disasters and political disruptions about four hundred years later, around 1200 B.C.E. We do not really know what happened, but all of the main archaeological sites show some evidence of destruction, burning, or hasty abandonment at about that time, and a sharp decline thereafter in the ambition and complexity of their material culture. Among these is the site of Troy itself, which was discovered in the late nineteenth century by Heinrich Schliemann, who followed the topographical details given in the *Iliad;* through this discovery, Schliemann both vindicated the historical validity of Homer and helped to found the field of archaeology.

Related in some way to the disruptions that ended the Bronze Age was the emergence of a new group of Greek-speakers as the dominant people on the mainland. The Classical Greeks referred to these people as the Dorians and believed that they had invaded Greece from the north. Modern historians are uncertain whether they were new migrants or people already present in Greece who newly came to power in the upheavals of this period. In any case, many people left the mainland as a consequence and moved east, settling on various islands of the Aegean and along the coast of Asia Minor, in the area that is now western Turkey but which then became, in its coastal region, as much a part of the Greek world as was the mainland itself.

Both the Greeks who remained on the mainland and those who migrated to Asia Minor lived in conditions that involved less material prosperity and less highly organized concentrations of political and military power than had been characteristic of the Mycenaean period, and their period is traditionally known as the Dark Age, both because their physical remains suggest a less magnificent level of civilization and because we know relatively little about it. One result of the transition to the Dark Age was that writing, which was probably practiced in the Mycenaean period only by a small class of professional scribes, fell out of use, and the Greeks became once again a culture without writing. On the other hand, they had always relied, and they continued to rely, on oral communication as their central means of recalling, preserving, and transmitting the historical memories, religious beliefs, and shared stories that in our culture would be committed to writing—or now to various forms of electronic media. In particular, the Greeks of Asia Minor, known as the Ionians, developed a tradition of heroic poetry through which they recalled their own history, looking back and recounting the experiences of that earlier, lost era. This poetry centered on certain legendary figures and events, among them the events surrounding the Trojan war, which, as mentioned above, appear to reflect the final moments of Mycenaean civilization.

The so-called Dark Age came to an end during a period roughly corresponding to the eighth century—the 700s—B.C.E. The cultural shift that we label the end of the Dark Age and the beginning of the Archaic Period involved not a series of upheavals, as with the end of the Bronze Age, but the emergence of new activity in a variety of fields. A growth in population led to a wave of colonization, with established Greek centers sending out colonies to such places as the Black Sea, Sicily, southern Italy, and southern France. There was also greater contact among the various Greek communities, which were politically distinct and remained so for centuries. This led to the development of institutions designed to unite those communities culturally and to reinforce a shared Greek, or Panhellenic, heritage, such as the oracle of Apollo at Delphi and the Olympic Games (founded in 776 B.C.E.). Around this time, the Greeks began to build large-scale temples and to make large-scale statues

and a new kind of pottery decorated with elaborate geometric pat-
terns. Many of the features of Greek culture that we associate with
the Classical Period—the period that loosely corresponds to the fifth
and fourth centuries B.C.E.—had their origins in the eighth century.

In addition to colonization, this was also a time of renewed
trade and thus of encounters with other Mediterranean cultures.
One consequence of this trade was that the Greeks came into con-
tact with the Phoenicians, a Semitic people whose culture was cen-
tered in present-day Lebanon, and learned from them a system of
writing—not a syllabary like Linear B, but an alphabet, the alphabet
which, with some modification, is still used to write Greek and
which eventually was adapted to become the Roman alphabet, now
widely used for many languages, including English.

This new way of writing Greek quickly became much more
widespread than Linear B had been, and it was put to a greater vari-
ety of uses, among them the writing down of poetry. Thus the *Iliad*
and other early Greek poems (including the other Homeric epic, the
*Odyssey*; two poems by Hesiod, the *Theogony* and *Works and Days*; and
a group of hymns that were also attributed to Homer in antiquity)
came into being in the written form in which we know them. But, as
mentioned already, while these poems were written down in the
eighth century, they claimed to describe events that had taken place
approximately five hundred years before. For the Greeks of the
eighth century and afterward, these were works of history, authorita-
tive records of their own past. A modern historian might be more
inclined to label them historical fiction, thinking that whatever con-
flict lies behind the story of the Trojan war is more likely to have
been fought over trade routes to the Black Sea than—as Homer tells
it—over the Trojans' theft from the Greeks of the world's most
beautiful woman, Helen of Troy. In any case, like most works of his-
torical fiction—or indeed of history—the *Iliad* and the *Odyssey* reflect
the time (or, in this case, the times) of their telling at least as much as
the time in which they are set.

Historians and archaeologists who have tried to match the
culture described in the Homeric epics to what we know of Greek
history from other sources have found that that culture unself-
consciously combines elements of the Bronze Age with elements of
the Dark Age: memories of the earlier time in which the Trojan leg-
end is set have been woven together with circumstances borrowed

from the period during which the legend evolved. This can be seen in the depictions of combat that are a major feature of the *Iliad*. While it is repeatedly mentioned that the weapons being used are made of bronze—which fell out of use for weapons after the Bronze Age, being replaced by iron—some of the specific implements and fighting practices belong to a later time. Some of the fighting practices described there seem not to be fully understood by the poet— for example, the use of chariots, which are mentioned mainly as transportation to and from the battle, when they must in fact have been used in the actual fighting.

The peacetime world, described more fully in the *Odyssey* than in the *Iliad*, centers on kingdoms that are much smaller and much less highly organized than those of the Mycenaean Period, and many details of their material culture and social organization accord more closely to what we know of Dark Age life. There are also ways in which the world of Homer reflects the emerging concerns and conditions of the eighth century: for example, some scholars draw a connection between the fact that the Homeric poems omit certain religious practices that were tied to particular localities and the unifying, Panhellenic impulses reflected in the Delphic Oracle and the Olympic Games. There is surely a connection to be made between the *Iliad*'s focus on the hard-won success of the Greeks in overcoming internal dissension to achieve the common goal of taking Troy and that period's concern with the development of a shared cultural identity. It is also clear that some of the practices of Homeric culture are entirely artificial, conditioned by the aims of the poem itself; for example, the habit that the *Iliad*'s heroes have of pausing in the middle of battle to talk, reflecting, as Sarpedon does, on the meaning of what they are doing—a fatal lapse in real combat, but an effective strategy for a poem.

## The Poetic Tradition

Just as the society described in the Homeric epics reflects the centuries-long period during which the Trojan legend evolved, so the poems themselves—in their language, their style, and their modes of narration—also reflect that period and that process of evolution. The *Iliad* is manifestly the product of a long tradition within Greek culture and follows on many previous tellings of the same legendary material. Beyond that, the poem has roots in the traditions of the ancient Near East, which we can recognize but not trace precisely. This can be seen in the parallels between episodes in the *Iliad* and many Near Eastern myths, such as the story told in the Sumerian *Epic of Gilgamesh*, which also concerns a hero who is the son of a goddess and who causes the death of his dearest companion, for whom he passionately grieves.

The *Iliad*'s debt to tradition is revealed in the way in which it tells its story, plunging into the quarrel of Achilles and Agamemnon with confidence that its audience will already be familiar with these characters and the legends to which they belong. Similarly, the characters in the poem—especially older characters like Nestor and Phoenix—habitually refer to other similar legends, apparently drawing on a related fund of inherited stories. The traditional character of Homeric poetry is also deeply embedded in the language and style of the original Greek text, as the scholarship of the last century has made increasingly clear. In particular, it has been demonstrated that the diction and phraseology of Homeric Greek are not those of written literature, but rather of the kind of orally composed and recited poetry that preceded our written *Iliad* and that still exists in some cultures today. Generally speaking, rather than reciting a fixed, memorized text, an oral poet composes a new telling of the story while speaking, always fitting the words into the patterns of a metrical scheme. To do this requires a different and larger set of verbal resources than those of writing or ordinary speech. A major achievement of Homeric scholarship—and especially of an American scholar of the 1920s and 1930s, Milman Parry, who did comparative work with the practicing oral poets of the Balkan region—has been to identify the peculiarities of Homeric Greek, which include an expanded vocabulary and a huge repertory of repeated phrases and lines, with the resources of the oral poet.

The identification of Homeric style as that of oral poetry has solved some of the problems that students of Homer wrestled with for centuries, as they tried to make sense of the ways in which the Homeric epics are unlike later written poems, in particular their continual use of repetition and their occasional rough edges and narrative inconsistencies. But it does not, of course, explain the *Iliad* we have, which is not an oral recitation, but a written text, although it should be stressed that, even after the *Iliad* was written down, it continued to be recited for centuries, at least into the Classical Period, and oral performance continued to be the medium through which this poem reached its primary audience, despite the existence of a written text.

Certain characteristics of the *Iliad* cannot easily be referred to the poem's oral origins, particularly its monumental scale. A performance of the *Iliad* would take at the absolute minimum about twenty hours, whereas the bards studied by modern scholars, like the several bards who are portrayed in the *Odyssey* as entertaining groups of people at banquets, all sing songs lasting about an hour. It is difficult, even impossible, to imagine an occasion when the *Iliad* could have been sung through for an audience from beginning to end. Clearly, it is significant that the final stages of the poem's composition coincide with the reintroduction of writing in the eighth century, but the exact role of writing in shaping the poem that we have remains mysterious, especially since marks of oral composition such as those found in Homer tend to disappear quite quickly once poets begin to use writing as an aid to composition.

Homeric scholars also have to deal with a further mystery, which is the relationship between the versions of these poems that we hypothesize were written down in the eighth century and the first written versions we have any evidence for: versions that were produced in the mainland city of Athens in the sixth century B.C.E. Just as we cannot disentangle the layers of previous history that merged in the written poems of the eighth century, we cannot altogether distinguish the further transformations that those poems underwent before they became the medieval manuscripts on which the texts we currently use—and ultimately this translation—are based. We do know, for example, that the division of the poems into books belongs to the third century B.C.E., when the poems were edited by scholars attached to the library of Alexandria in Egypt. But we are not sure what features may have been introduced, for example, when the poems were recorded in sixth-century Athens. The *Iliad* contained in this book is the product of four millennia—from the remembered experiences of the Mycenaean Period to the English words and phrases chosen by a late-twentieth-century translator.

Perhaps the greatest challenge posed by our awareness of the oral background of Homeric poetry is the issue of how to integrate the role of tradition into an appreciation of a poem that we view as an accomplished masterpiece. This is the problem that most excites present-day critics of Homer, who may find there an echo of the questions about the relative values of individual insight and inherited wisdom, or of personal achievement and collective action, that are central to the *Iliad* itself. Readers of the *Iliad* have to decide to what extent they are able to see it as the group effort of many generations, as opposed to the original creation of an individual.

It is notable in this context that the poet-narrator of the *Iliad* does not present himself as original, but rather as the mouthpiece, not of human tradition, but of divinities, the Muses. In doing so, he claims a far greater value for his work than he could if he presented it as his own invention, for the Muses' inspiration allows him to give a truthful account of past events that he has not witnessed, to produce a work of authoritative history. Nonetheless, most modern readers have found it difficult to view the *Iliad* and the *Odyssey* as anything other than the creations of an individual (or a pair of individuals). To many it is impossible to imagine that the qualities that make these poems so great—their fundamental coherence of design and theme, their profound and particular vision—could be anything other than the achievement of an unusually creative individual.

In attributing the *Iliad* to an individual, modern readers are also, of course, aligning themselves with ancient tradition. But the information we are given about Homer is quite unhelpful, consisting essentially of legends about a blind bard from an Ionian city (several claimed him) who wandered from place to place, having adventures suspiciously similar to those of his hero Odysseus. Modern critics tend to discount these legends and to find their version of Homer in the person responsible for whatever strikes them as the most impressive features of the epics: their monumental scale, their coherence of design, their written form, their reinterpretation of traditional material.

Much recent critical and scholarly work on the *Iliad* and the *Odyssey* has been devoted to this last feature, the reinterpretation of traditional material, showing how these poems employ traditional elements, but in purposeful, particular, and even untraditional ways. The fundamental decision to tell the Trojan legend through the brief episode of Achilles' rage is clearly one example of this: it not only allows the poet to bring concentration and intensity to what might otherwise be a sprawling narrative, but it helps him to ask fundamental questions about how the stories of individuals like Achilles fit into the larger projects of their communities.

Many studies have been devoted to showing how typical episodes that clearly reflect long-standing conventions of epic narrative are reworked in the *Iliad*, with striking and novel effects. For example, the typical scene of a hero arming for war is used with pointed significance to tell the story of Achilles. When Patroclus prepares for battle by putting on Achilles' armor, this is described in completely conventional terms, until the point at which the hero regularly picks up his spear, when we are given the ominous information that Patroclus did *not* pick up Achilles' spear, because he was, in fact, unable to lift it. When Achilles finally arms himself to avenge Patroclus' death, the momentousness of this entry into battle is expressed in the way in which the description of the decoration on a hero's shield—usually only a matter of several lines—is elaborated into a panorama of human activity that encompasses and subsumes the world in which the *Iliad*'s plot takes place.

Making use of what spotty evidence they have, scholars have attempted to reconstruct earlier versions of the stories or types of stories told in the *Iliad*, in order to show how they have been adapted to the *Iliad*'s distinctive purposes. Other versions of the Meleager story told by Phoenix in Book 9 allow us to see that there it has been reworked to provide a pointed parallel to the story of Achilles. Some critics have speculated that there may have been many traditional accounts of powerful heroes who felt dishonored and withdrew from their armies until their honor was restored, but that the surprising development of Achilles' continued withdrawal even after Agamemnon's embassy may have been unique to the *Iliad*. Our evidence suggests that other poems in the tradition out of which the *Iliad* and *Odyssey* emerged contained many more supernatural and miraculous elements, including the achievement of immortality by the most successful heroes. By contrast, the Homeric epics seem distinctive in their unremitting insistence on the constraints of mortal existence and the inescapability of death.

In making this translation, Stanley Lombardo has located Homer in the performer or performers through whom the *Iliad* existed primarily as a spoken work, even after it was written down. Lombardo's version highlights the living connection that the poet builds between himself and his audience and his evocation of the spontaneous and idiosyncratic accents of the individual speakers whom he impersonates. In doing so, Lombardo brings out yet another way in which the concerns of the poet intersect with those of his characters, for in his re-creation of heroic warfare, Homer has made it a realm not only of forceful action, but also of powerful speaking. The characters of the *Iliad* use speech constantly, to further their competitions through insults, to confer honor on one another through praise, to reflect on what they are doing, to bring the traditions of the past to bear on their present dilemmas, to lament their dead. In this way they fulfill the vision of heroism that Phoenix instilled in Achilles on the instructions of his father, Peleus: "To be a speaker of words and a doer of deeds" (9.455).

Sheila Murnaghan
University of Pennsylvania

# A Note on the Translation

The poetics of this translation of Homer's *Iliad* are easily and briefly stated: rhythms and language drawn from natural speech, in the tradition of American poetry; emphasis on the physicality, rapidity, and suppleness of the verse; varied treatment of epithets and formulae, often heightening their effect as poetic events; treatment of similes as partially independent poetic moments, indicated by italics and indentation; close attention to presentation of the text on the page; commitment to the poetic line. Above all, this translation reflects the oral performance nature of the original poems. The translation began as scripts for performance, and it has been shaped by the complementary pressures of poetic composition and oral performance. Throughout the period of composing the translation as poetry on the page, I continued reciting it to audiences, voicing the text as I crafted it and crafting it to capture the voice that I heard.

Stanley Lombardo
University of Kansas

# A Note on the Abridgment

Homer's *Iliad* is presented here in a version approximately one-third as long as the original poem. The passages that have been retained appear exactly as in the original Lombardo translation and have not been condensed or digested in any way. Omitted passages are indicated by book and line number and are summarized very briefly. The selections have been made with an eye toward keeping the major characters, events, and themes in clear focus.

# ILIAD 1

Rage:
             Sing, Goddess, Achilles' rage,
Black and murderous, that cost the Greeks
Incalculable pain, pitched countless souls
Of heroes into Hades' dark,
And left their bodies to rot as feasts                                  5
For dogs and birds, as Zeus' will was done.
    Begin with the clash between Agamemnon—
The Greek warlord—and godlike Achilles.

Which of the immortals set these two
At each other's throats?                                               10
                                 Apollo,
Zeus' son and Leto's, offended
By the warlord. Agamemnon had dishonored
Chryses, Apollo's priest, so the god
Struck the Greek camp with plague,                                     15
And the soldiers were dying of it.
                                 Chryses
Had come to the Greek beachhead camp
Hauling a fortune for his daughter's ransom.
Displaying Apollo's sacral ribbons                                     20
On a golden staff, he made a formal plea
To the entire Greek army, but especially
The commanders, Atreus' two sons:

"Sons of Atreus and Greek heroes all:
May the gods on Olympus grant you plunder                              25
Of Priam's city and a safe return home.
But give me my daughter back and accept
This ransom out of respect for Zeus' son,

Lord Apollo, who deals death from afar."

A murmur rippled through the ranks:                                    30
"Respect the priest and take the ransom."
But Agamemnon was not pleased
And dismissed Chryses with a rough speech:

"Don't let me ever catch you, old man, by these ships again,
Skulking around now or sneaking back later.                          35
The god's staff and ribbons won't save you next time.
The girl is mine, and she'll be an old woman in Argos
Before I let her go, working the loom in my house
And coming to my bed, far from her homeland.
Now clear out of here before you make me angry!"                     40

The old man was afraid and did as he was told.
He walked in silence along the whispering surf line,
And when he had gone some distance the priest
Prayed to Lord Apollo, son of silken-haired Leto:

"Hear me, Silverbow, Protector of Chryse,                            45
Lord of Holy Cilla, Master of Tenedos,
And Sminthian God of Plague!
If ever I've built a temple that pleased you
Or burnt fat thighbones of bulls and goats—
    Grant me this prayer:                                            50
Let the Danaans pay for my tears with your arrows!"

Apollo heard his prayer and descended Olympus' crags
Pulsing with fury, bow slung over one shoulder,
The arrows rattling in their case on his back
As the angry god moved like night down the mountain.                 55

He settled near the ships and let loose an arrow.
Reverberation from his silver bow hung in the air.
He picked off the pack animals first, and the lean hounds,
But then aimed his needle-tipped arrows at the men
And shot until the death-fires crowded the beach.                    60

Nine days the god's arrows rained death on the camp.
On the tenth day Achilles called an assembly.
Hera, the white-armed goddess, planted the thought in him
Because she cared for the Greeks and it pained her
To see them dying. When the troops had all mustered,            65
Up stood the great runner Achilles, and said:

"Well, Agamemnon, it looks as if we'd better give up
And sail home—assuming any of us are left alive—
If we have to fight both the war and this plague.
But why not consult some prophet or priest                      70
Or a dream interpreter, since dreams too come from Zeus,
Who could tell us why Apollo is so angry,
If it's for a vow or a sacrifice he holds us at fault.
Maybe he'd be willing to lift this plague from us
If he savored the smoke from lambs and prime goats."            75

Achilles had his say and sat down. Then up rose
Calchas, son of Thestor, bird-reader supreme,
Who knew what is, what will be, and what has been.
He had guided the Greek ships to Troy
Through the prophetic power Apollo                               80
Had given him, and he spoke out now:

"Achilles, beloved of Zeus, you want me to tell you
About the rage of Lord Apollo, the Arch-Destroyer.
And I will tell you. But you have to promise me and swear
You will support me and protect me in word and deed.           85
I have a feeling I might offend a person of some authority
Among the Greeks, and you know how it is when a king
Is angry with an underling. He might swallow his temper
For a day, but he holds it in his heart until later
And it all comes out. Will you guarantee my security?"         90

Achilles, the great runner, responded:

"Don't worry. Prophesy to the best of your knowledge.
I swear by Apollo, to whom you pray when you reveal
The gods' secrets to the Greeks, Calchas, that while I live

And look upon this earth, no one will lay a hand          95
On you here beside these hollow ships, no, not even
Agamemnon, who boasts he is the best of the Achaeans."

And Calchas, the perfect prophet, taking courage:

"The god finds no fault with vow or sacrifice.
It is for his priest, whom Agamemnon dishonored          100
And would not allow to ransom his daughter,
That Apollo deals and will deal death from afar.
He will not lift this foul plague from the Greeks
Until we return the dancing-eyed girl to her father
Unransomed, unbought, and make formal sacrifice          105
On Chryse. Only then might we appease the god."

He finished speaking and sat down. Then up rose
Atreus' son, the warlord Agamemnon,
Furious, anger like twin black thunderheads seething
In his lungs, and his eyes flickered with fire          110
As he looked Calchas up and down, and said:

                         "You damn soothsayer!
You've never given me a good omen yet.
You take some kind of perverse pleasure in prophesying
Doom, don't you? Not a single favorable omen ever!          115
Nothing good ever happens! And now you stand here
Uttering oracles before the Greeks, telling us
That your great ballistic god is giving us all this trouble
Because I was unwilling to accept the ransom
For Chryses' daughter but preferred instead to keep her          120
In my tent! And why shouldn't I? I like her better than
My wife Clytemnestra. She's no worse than her
When it comes to looks, body, mind, or ability.
Still, I'll give her back, if that's what's best.
I don't want to see the army destroyed like this.          125
But I want another prize ready for me right away.
I'm not going to be the only Greek without a prize,
It wouldn't be right. And you all see where mine is going."

And Achilles, strong, swift, and godlike:

"And where do you think, son of Atreus,                               130
You greedy glory-hound, the magnanimous Greeks
Are going to get another prize for you?
Do you think we have some kind of stockpile in reserve?
Every town in the area has been sacked and the stuff all divided.
You want the men to count it all back and redistribute it?       135
All right, you give the girl back to the god. The army
Will repay you three and four times over—when and if
Zeus allows us to rip Troy down to its foundations."

The warlord Agamemnon responded:

"You may be a good man in a fight, Achilles,                           140
And look like a god, but don't try to put one over on me—
It won't work. So while you have your prize,
You want me to sit tight and do without?
Give the girl back, just like that? Now maybe
If the army, in a generous spirit, voted me                              145
Some suitable prize of their own choice, something fair—
But if it doesn't, I'll just go take something myself,
Your prize perhaps, or Ajax's, or Odysseus',
And whoever she belongs to, it'll stick in his throat.

But we can think about that later.                                           150
                                    Right now we launch
A black ship on the bright salt water, get a crew aboard,
Load on a hundred bulls, and have Chryseis board her too,
My girl with her lovely cheeks. And we'll want a good man
For captain, Ajax or Idomeneus or godlike Odysseus—               155
Or maybe you, son of Peleus, our most formidable hero—
To offer sacrifice and appease the Arch-Destroyer for us."

Achilles looked him up and down and said:

"You sorry, profiteering excuse for a commander!
How are you going to get any Greek warrior                            160
To follow you into battle again? You know,

*I* don't have any quarrel with the Trojans,
They didn't do anything to *me* to make me
Come over here and fight, didn't run off *my* cattle or horses
Or ruin *my* farmland back home in Phthia, not with all          165
The shadowy mountains and moaning seas between.
It's for *you*, dogface, for your precious pleasure—
And Menelaus' honor—that we came here,
A fact you don't have the decency even to mention!
And now you're threatening to take away the prize             170
That I sweated for and the Greeks gave me.
I never get a prize equal to yours when the army
Captures one of the Trojan strongholds.
No, I do all the dirty work with my own hands,
And when the battle's over and we divide the loot            175
You get the lion's share and I go back to the ships
With some pitiful little thing, so worn out from fighting
I don't have the strength left even to complain.
Well, I'm going back to Phthia now. Far better
To head home with my curved ships than stay here,           180
Unhonored myself and piling up a fortune for you."

The warlord Agamemnon responded:

"Go ahead and desert, if that's what you want!
I'm not going to beg you to stay. There are plenty of others
Who will honor me, not least of all Zeus the Counselor.       185
To me, you're the most hateful king under heaven,
A born troublemaker. You actually *like* fighting and war.
If you're all that strong, it's just a gift from some god.
So why don't you go home with your ships and lord it over
Your precious Myrmidons. I couldn't care less about you        190
Or your famous temper. But I'll tell you this:
Since Phoebus Apollo is taking away my Chryseis,
Whom I'm sending back aboard ship with my friends,
I'm coming to your hut and taking Briseis,
Your own beautiful prize, so that you will see just how much    195
Stronger I am than you, and the next person will wince
At the thought of opposing me as an equal."

Achilles' chest was a rough knot of pain
Twisting around his heart: should he
Draw the sharp sword that hung by his thigh,                    *200*
Scatter the ranks and gut Agamemnon,
Or control his temper, repress his rage?
He was mulling it over, inching the great sword
From its sheath, when out of the blue
Athena came, sent by the white-armed goddess                    *205*
Hera, who loved and watched over both men.
She stood behind Achilles and grabbed his sandy hair,
Visible only to him: not another soul saw her.
Awestruck, Achilles turned around, recognizing
Pallas Athena at once—it was her eyes—                    *210*
And words flew from his mouth like winging birds:

"Daughter of Zeus! Why have you come here?
To see Agamemnon's arrogance, no doubt.
I'll tell you where I place my bets, Goddess:
Sudden death for this outrageous behavior."                    *215*

Athena's eyes glared through the sea's salt haze.

"I came to see if I could check this temper of yours,
Sent from heaven by the white-armed goddess
Hera, who loves and watches over both of you men.
Now come on, drop this quarrel, don't draw your sword.                    *220*
Tell him off instead. And I'll tell you,
Achilles, how things will be: You're going to get
Three times as many magnificent gifts
Because of his arrogance. Just listen to us and be patient."

Achilles, the great runner, responded:                    *225*

"When you two speak, Goddess, a man has to listen
No matter how angry. It's better that way.
Obey the gods and they hear you when you pray."

With that he ground his heavy hand
Onto the silver hilt and pushed the great sword                    *230*

Back into its sheath. Athena's speech
Had been well-timed. She was on her way
To Olympus by now, to the halls of Zeus
And the other immortals, while Achilles
Tore into Agamemnon again:                                        235

              "You bloated drunk,
With a dog's eyes and a rabbit's heart!
You've never had the guts to buckle on armor in battle
Or come out with the best fighting Greeks
On any campaign! Afraid to look Death in the eye,               240
Agamemnon? It's far more profitable
To hang back in the army's rear—isn't it?—
Confiscating prizes from any Greek who talks back
And bleeding your people dry. There's not a real man
Under your command, or this latest atrocity                       245
Would be your last, son of Atreus.
Now get this straight. I swear a formal oath:
   By this scepter, which will never sprout leaf
Or branch again since it was cut from its stock
In the mountains, which will bloom no more                       250
Now that bronze has pared off leaf and bark,
And which now the sons of the Greeks hold in their hands
At council, upholding Zeus' laws—
                         By this scepter I swear:
When every last Greek desperately misses Achilles,              255
Your remorse won't do any good then,
When Hector the man-killer swats you down like flies.
And you will eat your heart out
Because you failed to honor the best Greek of all."

Those were his words, and he slammed the scepter,              260
Studded with gold, to the ground and sat down.

Opposite him, Agamemnon fumed.
                         Then Nestor
Stood up, sweet-worded Nestor, the orator from Pylos
With a voice high-toned and liquid as honey.                     265
He had seen two generations of men pass away

In sandy Pylos and was now king in the third.
He was full of good will in the speech he made:

"It's a sad day for Greece, a sad day.
Priam and Priam's sons would be happy indeed,                    270
And the rest of the Trojans too, glad in their hearts,
If they learned all this about you two fighting,
Our two best men in council and in battle.
Now you listen to me, both of you. You are both
Younger than I am, and I've associated with men                    275
Better than you, and they didn't treat me lightly.
I've never seen men like those, and never will,
The likes of Peirithous and Dryas, a shepherd to his people,
Caineus and Exadius and godlike Polyphemus,
And Aegeus' son, Theseus, who could have passed for a god,                    280
The strongest men who ever lived on earth, the strongest,
And they fought with the strongest, with wild things
From the mountains, and beat the daylights out of them.
I was their companion, although I came from Pylos,
From the ends of the earth—they sent for me themselves.                    285
And I held my own fighting with them. You couldn't find
A mortal on earth who could fight with them now.
And when I talked in council, they took my advice.
So should you two now: taking advice is a good thing.
   Agamemnon, for all your nobility, do not take his girl.                    290
Leave her be: the army originally gave her to him as a prize.
Nor should you, son of Peleus, want to lock horns with a king.
A scepter-holding king has honor beyond the rest of men,
Power and glory given by Zeus himself.
You are stronger, and it is a goddess who bore you.                    295
But he is more powerful, since he rules over more.
Son of Atreus, cease your anger. And I appeal
Personally to Achilles to control his temper, since he is,
For all Greeks, a mighty bulwark in this evil war."

And Agamemnon, the warlord:                    300

"Yes, old man, everything you've said is absolutely right.
But this man wants to be ahead of everyone else,

He wants to rule everyone, give orders to everyone,
Lord it over everyone, and he's not going to get away with it.
If the gods eternal made him a spearman, does that mean          *305*
They gave him permission to be insolent as well?"

And Achilles, breaking in on him:

"Ha, and think of the names people would call me
If I bowed and scraped every time you opened your mouth.
Try that on somebody else, but not on me.                       *310*
I'll tell you this, and you can stick it in your gut:
I'm not going to put up a fight on account of the girl.
You, all of you, gave her to me and you can all take her back.
But anything else of mine in my black sailing ship
You keep your goddamn hands off, you hear?                      *315*
Try it. Let everybody here see how fast
Your black blood boils up around my spear."

   So it was a stand-off, their battle of words,
And the assembly beside the Greek ships dissolved.
Achilles went back to the huts by his ships                     *320*
With Patroclus and his men. Agamemnon had a fast ship
Hauled down to the sea, picked twenty oarsmen,
Loaded on a hundred bulls due to the god, and had
        Chryses' daughter,
His fair-cheeked girl, go aboard also. Odysseus captained,
And when they were all on board, the ship headed out to sea.    *325*

Onshore, Agamemnon ordered a purification.
The troops scrubbed down and poured the filth
Into the sea. Then they sacrificed to Apollo
Oxen and goats by the hundreds on the barren shore.
The smoky savor swirled up to the sky.                          *330*

That was the order of the day. But Agamemnon
Did not forget his spiteful threat against Achilles.
He summoned Talthybius and Eurybates,
Faithful retainers who served as his heralds:

"Go to the hut of Achilles, son of Peleus;                    335
Bring back the girl, fair-cheeked Briseis.
If he won't give her up, I'll come myself
With my men and take her—and freeze his heart cold."

It was not the sort of mission a herald would relish.
The pair trailed along the barren seashore                    340
Until they came to the Myrmidons' ships and encampment.
They found Achilles sitting outside his hut
Beside his black ship. He was not glad to see them.
They stood respectfully silent, in awe of this king,
And it was Achilles who was moved to address them first:      345

"Welcome, heralds, the gods' messengers and men's.
Come closer. You're not to blame, Agamemnon is,
Who sent you here for the girl, Briseis.
                                        Patroclus,
Bring the girl out and give her to these gentlemen.          350
You two are witnesses before the blessed gods,
Before mortal men and that hard-hearted king,
If ever I'm needed to protect the others
From being hacked to bits. His mind is murky with anger,
And he doesn't have the sense to look ahead and behind       355
To see how the Greeks might defend their ships."

Thus Achilles.
                Patroclus obeyed his beloved friend
And brought Briseis, cheeks flushed, out of the tent
And gave her to the heralds, who led her away.              360
She went unwillingly.
                Then Achilles, in tears,
Withdrew from his friends and sat down far away
On the foaming white seashore, staring out
At the endless sea. Stretching out his hands,             365
He prayed over and over to his beloved mother:

"Mother, since you bore me for a short life only,
Olympian Zeus was supposed to grant me honor.
Well, he hasn't given me any at all. Agamemnon

Has taken away my prize and dishonored me."                     370

His voice, choked with tears, was heard by his mother
As she sat in the sea-depths beside her old father.
She rose up from the white-capped sea like a mist,
And settling herself beside her weeping child
She stroked him with her hand and talked to him:                375

"Why are you crying, son? What's wrong?
Don't keep it inside. Tell me so we'll both know."

And Achilles, with a deep groan:

"You already know. Why do I have to tell you?
We went after Thebes, Eëtion's sacred town,                      380
Sacked it and brought the plunder back here.
The army divided everything up and chose
For Agamemnon fair-cheeked Chryseis.
Then her father, Chryses, a priest of Apollo,
Came to our army's ships on the beachhead,                       385
Hauling a fortune for his daughter's ransom.
He displayed Apollo's sacral ribbons
On a golden staff and made a formal plea
To the entire Greek army, but especially
The commanders, Atreus' two sons.                                390
You could hear the troops murmuring,
'Respect the priest and take the ransom.'
But Agamemnon wouldn't hear of it
And dismissed Chryses with a rough speech.
The old man went back angry, and Apollo                          395
Heard his beloved priest's prayer.
He hit the Greeks hard, and the troops
Were falling over dead, the god's arrows
Raining down all through the Greek camp.
A prophet told us the Arch-Destroyer's will,                     400
And I demanded the god be appeased.
Agamemnon got angry, stood up
And threatened me, and made good his threat.
The high command sent the girl on a fast ship

Back to Chryse with gifts for Apollo,                    *405*
And heralds led away my girl, Briseis,
Whom the army had given to me.
Now you have to help me, if you can.
   Go to Olympus
And call in the debt that Zeus owes you.                 *410*
I remember often hearing you tell
In my father's house how you alone managed,
Of all the immortals, to save Zeus' neck
When the other Olympians wanted to bind him—
Hera and Poseidon and Pallas Athena.                     *415*
You came and loosened him from his chains,
And you lured to Olympus' summit the giant
With a hundred hands whom the gods call
Briareus but men call Aegaeon, stronger
Even than his own father Uranus, and he                  *420*
Sat hulking in front of cloud-black Zeus,
Proud of his prowess, and scared all the gods
Who were trying to put the son of Cronus in chains.
   Remind Zeus of this, sit holding his knees,
See if he is willing to help the Trojans                 *425*
Hem the Greeks in between the fleet and the sea.
Once they start being killed, the Greeks may
Appreciate Agamemnon for what he is,
And the wide-ruling son of Atreus will see
What a fool he's been because he did not honor           *430*
The best of all the fighting Achaeans."

And Thetis, now weeping herself:

"O my poor child. I bore you for sorrow,
Nursed you for grief. Why? You should be
Spending your time here by your ships                    *435*
Happily and untroubled by tears,
Since life is short for you, all too brief.
Now you're destined for both an early death
And misery beyond compare. It was for this
I gave birth to you in your father's palace              *440*
Under an evil star.

              I'll go to snow-bound Olympus
And tell all this to the Lord of Lightning.
I hope he listens. You stay here, though,
Beside your ships and let the Greeks feel                              445
Your spite; withdraw completely from the war.
Zeus left yesterday for the River Ocean
On his way to a feast with the Ethiopians.
All the gods went with him. He'll return
To Olympus twelve days from now,                                       450
And I'll go then to his bronze threshold
And plead with him. I think I'll persuade him."

And she left him there, angry and heartsick
At being forced to give up the silken-waisted girl.

   Meanwhile, Odysseus was putting in                      455
At Chryse with his sacred cargo on board.
When they were well within the deepwater harbor
They furled the sail and stowed it in the ship's hold,
Slackened the forestays and lowered the mast,
Working quickly, then rowed her to a mooring, where                   460
They dropped anchor and made the stern cables fast.
The crew disembarked on the seabeach
And unloaded the bulls for Apollo the Archer.
Then Chryses' daughter stepped off the seagoing vessel,
And Odysseus led her to an altar                                      465
And placed her in her father's hands, saying:

"Chryses, King Agamemnon has sent me here
To return your child and offer to Phoebus
Formal sacrifice on behalf of the Greeks.
So may we appease Lord Apollo, and may he                             470
Lift the afflictions he has sent upon us."

Chryses received his daughter tenderly.

Moving quickly, they lined the hundred oxen
Around the massive altar, a glorious offering,
Washed their hands and sprinkled on the victims                       475

Sacrificial barley. On behalf of the Greeks
Chryses lifted his hands and prayed aloud:

"Hear me, Silverbow, Protector of Chryse,
Lord of Holy Cilla, Master of Tenedos,
As once before you heard my prayer,                          *480*
Did me honor, and smote the Greeks mightily,
So now also grant me this prayer:
                                        Lift the plague
From the Greeks and save them from death."

Thus the old priest, and Apollo heard him.                   *485*

After the prayers and the strewing of barley
They slaughtered and flayed the oxen,
Jointed the thighbones and wrapped them
In a layer of fat with cuts of meat on top.
The old man roasted them over charcoal                       *490*
And doused them with wine. Younger men
Stood by with five-tined forks in their hands.
When the thigh pieces were charred and they had
Tasted the tripe, they cut the rest into strips,
Skewered it on spits and roasted it skillfully.             *495*
When they were done and the feast was ready,
Feast they did, and no one lacked an equal share.
When they had all had enough to eat and drink,
The young men topped off mixing bowls with wine
And served it in goblets to all the guests.                  *500*
All day long these young Greeks propitiated
The god with dancing, singing to Apollo
A paean as they danced, and the god was pleased.
When the sun went down and darkness came on,
They went to sleep by the ship's stern-cables.               *505*

Dawn came early, a palmetto of rose,
Time to make sail for the wide beachhead camp.
They set up mast and spread the white canvas,
And the following wind, sent by Apollo,
Boomed in the mainsail. An indigo wave                        *510*

Hissed off the bow as the ship surged on,
Leaving a wake as she held on course through the billows.

When they reached the beachhead they hauled the black ship
High on the sand and jammed in the long chocks;
Then the crew scattered to their own huts and ships.                    515

All this time Achilles, the son of Peleus in the line of Zeus,
Nursed his anger, the great runner idle by his fleet's fast hulls.
He was not to be seen in council, that arena for glory,
Nor in combat. He sat tight in camp consumed with grief,
His great heart yearning for the battle cry and war.                   520

   Twelve days went by. Dawn.
The gods returned to Olympus,
Zeus at their head.
                        Thetis did not forget
Her son's requests. She rose from the sea                              525
And up through the air to the great sky
And found Cronus' wide-seeing son
Sitting in isolation on the highest peak
Of the rugged Olympic massif.
She settled beside him, and touched his knees                          530
With her left hand, his beard with her right,
And made her plea to the Lord of Sky:

"Father Zeus, if I have ever helped you
In word or deed among the immortals,
   Grant me this prayer:                                               535
Honor my son, doomed to die young
And yet dishonored by King Agamemnon,
Who stole his prize, a personal affront.
Do justice by him, Lord of Olympus.
Give the Trojans the upper hand until the Greeks                       540
Grant my son the honor he deserves."

Zeus made no reply but sat a long time
In silence, clouds scudding around him.
Thetis held fast to his knees and asked again:

"Give me a clear yes or no. Either nod in assent 545
Or refuse me. Why should you care if I know
How negligible a goddess I am in your eyes."

This provoked a troubled, gloomy response:

"This is disastrous. You're going to force me
Into conflict with Hera. I can just hear her now, 550
Cursing me and bawling me out. As it is,
She already accuses me of favoring the Trojans.
Please go back the way you came. Maybe
Hera won't notice. I'll take care of this.
And so you can have some peace of mind, 555
I'll say yes to you by nodding my head,
The ultimate pledge. Unambiguous,
Irreversible, and absolutely fulfilled,
Whatever I say yes to with a nod of my head."

And the Son of Cronus nodded. Black brows 560
Lowered, a glory of hair cascaded down from the Lord's
Immortal head, and the holy mountain trembled.

Their conference over, the two parted. The goddess
Dove into the deep sea from Olympus' snow-glare
And Zeus went to his home. The gods all 565
Rose from their seats at their father's entrance. Not one
Dared watch him enter without standing to greet him.
And so God entered and took his high seat.
                                        But Hera
Had noticed his private conversation with Thetis, 570
The silver-footed daughter of the Old Man of the Sea,
And flew at him with cutting words:

"Who was that you were scheming with just now?
You just love devising secret plots behind my back,
Don't you? You can't bear to tell me what you're thinking, 575
Or you don't dare. Never have and never will."

The Father of Gods and Men answered:

"Hera, don't hope to know all my secret thoughts.
It would strain your mind even though you are my wife.
What it is proper to hear, no one, human or divine,                    *580*
Will hear before you. But what I wish to conceive
Apart from the other gods, don't pry into that."

And Lady Hera, with her oxen eyes wide:

"Oh my. The awesome son of Cronus has spoken.
Pry? You know that I never pry. And you always                    *585*
Cheerfully volunteer—whatever information you please.
It's just that I have this feeling that somehow
The silver-footed daughter of the Old Man of the Sea
May have won you over. She *was* sitting beside you
Up there in the mist, and she did touch your knees.                    *590*
And I'm pretty sure that you agreed to honor Achilles
And destroy Greeks by the thousands beside their ships."

And Zeus, the master of cloud and storm:

"You witch! Your intuitions are always right.
But what does it get you? Nothing, except that                    *595*
I like you less than ever. And so you're worse off.
If it's as you think it is, it's my business, not yours.
So sit down and shut up and do as I say.
You see these hands? All the gods on Olympus
Won't be able to help you if I ever lay them on you."                    *600*

Hera lost her nerve when she heard this.
She sat down in silence, fear cramping her heart,
And gloom settled over the gods in Zeus' hall.
Hephaestus, the master artisan, broke the silence,
Out of concern for his ivory-armed mother:                    *605*

"This is terrible; it's going to ruin us all.
If you two quarrel like this over mortals
It's bound to affect us gods. There'll be no more
Pleasure in our feasts if we let things turn ugly.
Mother, please, I don't have to tell you,                    *610*

You have to be pleasant to our father Zeus
So he won't be angry and ruin our feast.
If the Lord of Lightning wants to blast us from our seats,
He can—that's how much stronger he is.
So apologize to him with silken-soft words,                    615
And the Olympian in turn will be gracious to us."

He whisked up a two-handled cup, offered it
To his dear mother, and said to her:

"I know it's hard, Mother, but you have to endure it.
I don't want to see you getting beat up, and me               620
Unable to help you. The Olympian can be rough.
Once before when I tried to rescue you
He flipped me by my foot off our balcony.
I fell all day and came down when the sun did
On the island of Lemnos, scarcely alive.                       625
The Sintians had to nurse me back to health."

By the time he finished, the ivory-armed goddess
Was smiling at her son. She accepted the cup from him.
Then the lame god turned serving boy, siphoning nectar
From the mixing bowl and pouring the sweet liquor             630
For all of the gods, who couldn't stop laughing
At the sight of Hephaestus hustling through the halls.

And so all day long until the sun went down
They feasted to their hearts' content,
Apollo playing beautiful melodies on the lyre,                 635
The Muses singing responsively in lovely voices.
And when the last gleams of sunset had faded,
They turned in for the night, each to a house
Built by Hephaestus, the renowned master craftsman,
The burly blacksmith with the soul of an artist.              640

And the Lord of Lightning, Olympian Zeus, went to his bed,
The bed he always slept in when sweet sleep overcame him.
He climbed in and slept, next to golden-throned Hera.

# ILIAD 2

The gods slept soundly that night,
And the men, by their warhorses.

But Zeus lay awake in the dark,
Thinking of how to honor Achilles
And destroy Greeks by the shipload.                          5
His thoughts parted like stormclouds,
And in the clear space between them
He saw what seemed to be the best plan:
To send to Agamemnon, son of Atreus,
A wooly menace, a Dream,                                    10
And to it he spoke these feathery words:

"Go, deadly Dream, along the Greek ships
Until you come to the hut of Agamemnon,
And deliver this message to him exactly:
Order him to arm his long-haired Greeks.                    15
Now is his time to capture Troy.
The Olympian gods are no longer divided;
Hera has bent them all to her will
And targeted the Trojans for pain."

The Dream listened and went. Shadows flew                   20
Around the Greek ships. It found Agamemnon
Wrapped in deep, starlit slumber.

The Dream stood above his head. It looked
Like Nestor, the old man that Agamemnon
Respected the most, looked just like Nestor,                25
And this dream that was a god addressed the king:

"Asleep, son of Atreus, horsebreaker,
Wise man? You can't sleep all night.
All those decisions to make, so many people

Depending on you. I'll be brief.                              *30*
I am a messenger from Zeus, who is
Far away, but loves you and pities you.
He orders you to arm your long-haired Greeks.
Now is your time to capture Troy.
The Olympian gods are no longer divided;                      *35*
Hera has bent them all to her will
And targeted Troy for sorrow from Zeus.
Think it over. Keep your wits about you,
And don't forget this when sleep slips away."

And the voice trailed off, leaving him there                  *40*
Dreaming of things that were never to be.
He thought he would take Priam's city that day,
The fool. He didn't know what Zeus had in mind,
The pain and groans for both Trojans and Greeks
In the unendurable crush of battle.                           *45*
He woke from sleep, the god's voice
Eddying around him. He sat upright,
Pulled on a silky shirt, threw on a cloak,
Laced a pair of sandals on his shining feet,
And hung from his shoulder a silver-worked sword.             *50*
And he held his imperishable, ancestral staff
As he walked through the ships of the bronze-kilted Greeks.

Dawn had just reached the peak of Olympus,
Speaking light to Zeus and the other immortals.

[Lines 55–225 are omitted. Agamemnon tests the troops' morale by sug-
gesting that they lift the siege and sail for home. They are barely restrained
from doing so by Odysseus, who brings them back to assembly.]

And so Odysseus mastered the army. The men all
Streamed back from their ships and huts and assembled
With a roar.

    *A wave from the restless, churning sea*
  *Crashes on a beach, and the water seethes and thunders.*        *230*

They had all dropped to the sand and were sitting there,
Except for one man, Thersites, a blathering fool
And a rabble rouser. This man had a repertory
Of choice insults he used at random to revile the nobles,
Saying anything he thought the soldiers would laugh at.          235
He was also the ugliest soldier at the siege of Troy,
Bowlegged, walked with a limp, his shoulders
Slumped over his caved-in chest, and up top
Scraggly fuzz sprouted on his pointy head.
Achilles especially hated him, as did Odysseus,              240
Because he was always provoking them. Now
He was screaming abuse at Agamemnon.
The Achaeans were angry with him and indignant,
But that didn't stop him from razzing the warlord:

"What's wrong, son of Atreus, something you need?            245
Your huts are filled with bronze, and with women
We Achaeans pick out and give to you first of all
Whenever we take some town. Are you short of gold?
Maybe some Trojan horse breeder will bring you some
Out of Ilion as ransom for his son                          250
Whom I or some other Achaean has captured.
Maybe it's a young girl for you to make love to
And keep off somewhere for yourself. It's not right
For a leader to march our troops into trouble.
You Achaeans are a disgrace, Achaean women, not men!        255
Let's sail home in our ships and leave him here
To stew over his prizes so he'll have a chance to see
Whether he needs our help or not. Furthermore,
He dishonored Achilles, who's a much better man.
Achilles doesn't have an angry bone in his body,            260
Or this latest atrocity would be your last, son of Atreus!"

That was the abuse Agamemnon took
From the mouth of Thersites. Odysseus
Was on him in a flash, staring him down
With a scowl, and laid into him:                            265

"Mind your tongue, Thersites. Better think twice

About being the only man here to quarrel with his betters.
I don't care how bell-toned an orator you are,
You're nothing but trash. There's no one lower
In all the army that followed Agamemnon to Troy.                    270
You have no right even to mention kings in public,
Much less badmouth them so you can get to go home.
We have no idea how things are going to turn out,
What kind of homecoming we Achaeans will have.
Yet you have the nerve to revile Agamemnon,                         275
Son of Atreus, the shepherd of his people,
Because the Danaan heroes are generous to him?
You think you can stand up in public and insult him?
Well, let me tell you something. I guarantee
That if I ever catch you running on at the mouth again             280
As you were just now, my name isn't Odysseus
And may I never again be called Telemachus' father
If I don't lay hold of you, strip your ass naked,
And run you out of the assembly and through the ships,
Crying at all the ugly licks I land on you."                        285

And with that he whaled the staff down
On Thersites' back. The man crumpled in pain
And tears flooded his eyes. A huge bloody welt
Rose on his back under the gold stave's force,
And he sat there astounded, drooling with pain                      290
And wiping away his tears. The troops, forgetting
Their disappointment, had a good laugh
At his expense, looking at each other and saying:

"Oh man! You can't count how many good things
Odysseus has done for the Greeks, a real leader                     295
In council and in battle, but this tops them all,
The way he took that loudmouth out of commission.
I don't think he'll ever be man enough again
To rile the commanders with all his insults."

That's what they were saying in the ranks.                          300

*[Lines 301–471 are omitted. Odysseus and Nestor advance powerful argu-
ments for continuing the war.]*

The warlord Agamemnon
Ordered the heralds to muster the troops
In battle formation. They gave their skirling cry,
And all the commanders around Atreus' son                    475
Hurried to have their men fall in.
And in their midst Athena, eyes like slate,
Carried the aegis, priceless and out of all time,
Pure gold tassels flying in the wind, each
Woven strand worth a hundred oxen.                           480
And the goddess herself, glowing like moonlight,
Rushed over the sand, sweeping them on
And stiffening their hearts, so that for each of them
To die in battle was sweeter than going home.

*A fire raging through endless forests*                      485
*In a mountain range can be seen far away*
*As a distant glow.*

Likewise the glare
From the advancing army's unimaginable bronze,
An eerie light that reached the stratosphere.                490

*Migratory birds—cranes, geese, or long-necked swans—*
*Are gathering in a meadow in Asia*
*Where the river Caystrius branches out in streams.*
*For a while they fly in random patterns*
*For the pure joy of using their wings,*                     495
*But then with a single cry they start to land,*
*One line of birds settling in front of another*
*Until the whole meadow is a carpet of sound.*

Likewise from the ships and huts, tribe after tribe
Poured out onto the Scamander's floodplain,                  500
And the ground groaned and reverberated
Under their feet and the hooves of their horses.

And they stood in the flowering meadow there,
Countless as leaves, or as flowers in their season.

> *Innumerable throngs of buzzing flies*          505
> *Will swarm all over a herdsman's yard*
> *In springtime, when milk wets the pails—*

Likewise the throngs of long-haired Greeks
Who stood on the plain facing the Trojans,
Intent on hammering them to pieces.          510

> *And as goatherds easily separate out*
> *Wide flocks of goats mingled in pasture,*

So the commanders drew up their troops
To enter battle, and Lord Agamemnon
Moved among them like Zeus himself,          515
The look in his eyes, the carriage of his head,
With a torso like Ares', or like Poseidon's.

> *Picture a bull that stands out from the herd*
> *Head and horns above the milling cattle—*

Zeus on that day made the son of Atreus          520
A man who stood out from the crowd of heroes.

[Lines 522–872 are omitted. In a passage known as the Catalogue of the
Ships, the poet lists the contingents of the Greek army and their leaders.]

But tell me now, Muse, who were the best
Of men and of horses in the Atreides' army?

The best horses were the mares of Eumelus,          875
Swift as birds, of the same age, with matching coats,
And their backs were as even as a levelling line.
Apollo Silverbow had bred them in Pereia,
A team of mares who bore Panic in battle.

The best warrior was Telamonian Ajax—                      *880*
While Achilles was in his rage. For Achilles
Was second to no one, as were the horses
That bore Peleus' flawless son. But now he lay idle
Among his beaked, seagoing hulls, furious
With Agamemnon, the shepherd of the people,                 *885*
The son of Atreus. Achilles' men
Amused themselves on the shore, throwing
The discus and javelin and shooting their bows.
The horses stood beside their chariots
Champing lotus and marsh parsley.                           *890*
The chariots lay covered in their owners' huts.
The men missed their leader. They tramped
Through the camp and had no part in fighting.

  The army marched, and it was as though the land
Were swept with fire. Earth groaned beneath them,          *895*

  *As beneath Zeus when in his wrath he thunders*
  *And lashes the country of the Arimi with lightning*
  *Where men say Typhoeus lies in the ground.*

So the earth groaned under their feet
As they pressed on quickly over the plain.                 *900*

  Zeus notified the Trojans of all this
By sending Iris streaking down to Ilion.
She found the citizens assembled in one body,
Young and old alike, near Priam's gate, talking.
Iris positioned herself nearby                             *905*
And made her voice sound like Polites'—
A son of Priam who, trusting his speed,
Often sat as lookout on top of the barrow
Of old Aesytes, watching for any movement
Of Greek troops from their ships.                          *910*
Using his voice, the goddess said to Priam:

"Sir, you are as fond of endless speeches now
As you were in peacetime. But this is war.

I have been in a battle or two, but never
Have I seen an army like this,                              *915*
Covering the plain like leaves, or like sand,
As it advances to attack the city.
Hector, you're in charge of this operation.
But because there are so many allies here
With different languages from points abroad,                *920*
Each captain should give the word to his own men
And lead them out marshalled by cities."

Hector knew this was a goddess' speech
And dismissed the assembly. They rushed to arms.
All the gates were opened, and the troops                   *925*
Poured through them, on foot and in war cars.
In front of the city there is a steep hill
Out in the plain, level terrain all around it.
Men call this hill Batieia. Immortals call it
The barrow of Myrine the Dancer.                            *930*
It was here that the Trojans and their allies
Drew up their troops in companies.

*[The rest of Book 2 (lines 933–97) is omitted. The poet lists the contingents of the Trojan army.]*

# ILIAD 3

Two armies,
The troops in divisions
Under their commanders,

The Trojans advancing across the plain

*Like cranes beating their metallic wings*                    5
*In the stormy sky at winter's onset,*
*Unspeakable rain at their backs, their necks stretched*
*Toward Oceanic streams and down*
*To strafe the brown Pygmy race,*
*Bringing strife and bloodshed from the sky at dawn,*        10

While the Greeks moved forward in silence,
Their breath curling in long angry plumes
That acknowledged their pledges to die for each other.

*Banks of mist settle on mountain peaks*
*And seep into the valleys. Shepherds dislike it*            15
*But for a thief it is better than night,*
*And a man can see only as far as he can throw a stone.*

No more could the soldiers see through the cloud of dust
The armies tramped up as they moved through the plain.

And when they had almost closed—                            20
Was it a god?—no, not a god
But Paris who stepped out from the Trojan ranks,
Leopard skin on his shoulders, curved bow, sword,
And shaking two bronze-tipped spears at the Greeks
He invited their best to fight him to the death.            25

When Menelaus, who was Ares' darling, saw him
Strutting out from the ranks, he felt

> As a lion must feel when he finds the carcass
> Of a stag or wild goat, and, half-starving,
> Consumes it greedily even though hounds and hunters 30
> Are swarming down on him.

It was Paris all right,
Who could have passed for a god,
And Menelaus grinned as he hefted his gear
And stepped down from his chariot. He would 35
Have his revenge at last. Paris' blood
Turned milky when he saw him coming on,
And he faded back into the Trojan troops
With cheeks as pale as if he had seen—
Had almost stepped on—a poisonous snake 40
In a mountain pass. He could barely stand
As disdainful Trojans made room for him in the ranks,
And Hector, seeing his brother tremble at Atreus' son,
Started in on him with these abusive epithets:

"Paris, you desperate, womanizing pretty boy! 45
I wish you had never been born, or had died unmarried.
Better that than this disgrace before the troops.
Can't you just hear it, the long-haired Greeks
Chuckling and saying that our champion wins
For good looks but comes up short on offense and defense? 50
Is this how you were when you got up a crew
And sailed overseas, hobnobbed with the warrior caste
In a foreign country and sailed off with
A beautiful woman with marriage ties to half of them?
You're nothing but trouble for your father and your city, 55
A joke to your enemies and an embarrassment to yourself.
No, don't stand up to Menelaus: you might find out
What kind of a man it is whose wife you're sleeping with.
You think your lyre will help you, or Aphrodite's gifts,
Your hair, your pretty face, when you sprawl in the dust? 60
It's the Trojans who are cowards, or you'd have long since
Been dressed out in stones for all the harm you've done."

And Paris, handsome as a god, answered him:

"That's only just, Hector. You've got a mind
Like an axe, you know, always sharp,                               65
Making the skilled cut through a ship's beam,
Multiplying force—nothing ever turns your edge.
But don't throw golden Aphrodite's gifts in my face.
We don't get to choose what the gods give us, you know,
And we can't just toss their gifts aside.                          70
So all right, if you want me to fight, fine.
Have the Trojans and the Greeks sit down,
And Menelaus and I will square off in the middle
To fight for Helen and all her possessions.
Winner take all.                                                  75
And everyone else will swear oaths of friendship,
You all to live here in the fertile Troad,
And they to go back to bluegrass Argos
And Achaea with its beautiful women."

Hector liked what he heard.                                        80
He went out in front along the Trojan ranks
Holding a spear broadside and made them all sit down.
Greek archers and slingers were taking aim at him
And already starting to shoot arrows and stones
When Agamemnon boomed out a command                                85
For them to hold their fire. Hector was signalling
That he had something to say, and his helmet
Caught the morning sun as he addressed both armies:

"Listen to me, Trojans, and you warriors from Greece.
Paris, on account of whom this war began, says this:              90
He wants all the Trojan and Greek combatants
To lay their weapons down on the ground.
He and Menelaus will square off in the middle
And fight for Helen and all her possessions.
Winner take all.                                                  95
And everyone else swears oaths of friendship."

Utter silence,
Until Menelaus, who was good at the war shout, said:

"Now listen to me, since my pain is paramount
In all this. It may be that the Greeks and Trojans          *100*
Can at last call it quits. We've had enough suffering
From this quarrel of mine that Paris began.
Whichever of us is due to die, let him die.
Then the rest of you can be done with each other.
Bring a pair of lambs, a white one and a black,            *105*
For Earth and Sun. Our side will bring another for Zeus.
And have Priam come, so he can swear oaths himself,
In person, since his sons are arrogant perjurers
Who would just as soon trample on Zeus' solemn word.
Younger men always have their heads in the clouds.         *110*
An old man looks ahead and behind, and the result
Is far better for both parties involved."

You could see their mood brighten,
Greeks and Trojans both, with the hope
That this wretched war would soon be over.                 *115*
They pulled their chariots up in rows,
Dismounted, and piled up their weapons.

There was not much space between the two armies.

Hector dispatched two heralds to the city
To fetch the lambs and summon Priam.                       *120*
Agamemnon sent Talthybius back to the ships
With orders to bring back a lamb.

While these human heralds were off on their missions,
Iris, the gods' herald (who is also the rainbow),
Came to white-armed Helen disguised as Laodice,           *125*
Her sister-in-law and Priam's most beautiful daughter.
She found Helen in the main hall, weaving a folding mantle
On a great loom and designing into the blood-red fabric
The trials that the Trojans and Greeks had suffered
For her beauty under Ares' murderous hands.                *130*
Iris stood near Helen and said:

"Come and see, dear lady, the amazing thing

The Greek and Trojan warriors have done.
They've fought all these years out on the plain,
Lusting for each other's blood, but now                          *135*
They've sat down in silence—halted the war—
They're leaning back on their shields
And their long spears are stuck in the sand.
But Paris and Menelaus are going to fight
A duel with lances, and the winner                               *140*
Will lay claim to you as his beloved wife."

The goddess' words turned Helen's mind
Into a sweet mist of desire
For her former husband, her parents, and her city.
She dressed herself in fine silvery linens                       *145*
And came out of her bedroom crying softly.
Two maids trailed behind, Aethrê,
Pittheus' daughter, and cow-eyed Clyménê.
They came to the Western Gate,
Where a knot of old men sat—                                     *150*

Priam, Panthous, Thymoetes,
Lampus, Clytius, Hicetaon
(Who was in Ares' bloodline),
Ucalegon and Antenor,
Who lived and breathed wisdom—                                   *155*

These veterans sat on the wall by the Western Gate,
Too old to fight now, but excellent counsellors.

> *Think of cicadas perched on a branch,*
> *Their delicate voices shrill in the woods.*

Such were the voices of these Trojan elders                      *160*
Sitting on the tower by the Western Gate.
When they saw Helen coming
Their rasping whispers flew along the wall:

"Who could blame either the Trojans or Greeks
For suffering so long for a woman like this."                    *165*

"Her eyes are not human."

"Whatever she is, let her go back with the ships
And spare us and our children a generation of pain."

But Priam called out to her:

"Come here, dear child, sit next to me                              *170*
So you can see your former husband
And dear kinsmen. You are not to blame
For this war with the Greeks. The gods are.
Now tell me, who is that enormous man
Towering over the Greek troops, handsome,                          *175*
Well-built? I've never laid eyes on such
A fine figure of a man. He looks like a king."

And Helen,
The sky's brightness reflected in her mortal face:

"Reverend you are to me dear father-in-law,                         *180*
A man to hold in awe. I'm so ashamed.
Death should have been a sweeter evil to me
Than following your son here, leaving my home,
My marriage, my friends, my precious daughter,
That lovely time in my life. None of it was to be,                  *185*
And lamenting it has been my slow death.
But you asked me something, and I'll answer.
That man is Agamemnon, son of Atreus,
A great king and a strong warrior both.
He was also my brother-in-law—shameless bitch                      *190*
That I am—if that life was ever real."

The old man was lost in reverie and wonder:

"The son of Atreus. Born to power and wealth.
Blessed by the gods. Now I see
How many Greek lads you command.                                   *195*
I thought I saw it all when I went
To Phrygia once and saw thousands

Of soldiers and gleaming horses
Under the command of Otreus and Mygdon
Massed by the banks of the Sangarios,                          *200*
An army in which I myself served
On that fateful day when the Amazons
Swept down to fight against men.
They were nothing compared to these wild-eyed Greeks."

Then he saw Odysseus and asked:                               *205*

"Now tell me about this one, dear child,
Shorter than Agamemnon by a head
But broader in the shoulders and chest.
His armor is lying on the ground
And he's roaming the ranks like a ram,                        *210*
That's it, just like a thick-fleeced ram
Striding through a flock of silvery sheep."

And Helen, Zeus' child:

                    "That is Laertes' son,
The master strategist Odysseus, born and bred                 *215*
In the rocky hills of Ithaca. He knows
Every trick there is, and his mind runs deep."

Antenor turned to her and observed astutely:

"Your words are not off the mark there, madam.
Odysseus came here once before, on an embassy                 *220*
For your sake along with Menelaus.
I entertained them courteously in the great hall
And learned each man's character and depth of mind.
Standing in a crowd of Trojans, Menelaus,
With his wide shoulders, was more prominent,                  *225*
But when both were seated Odysseus was lordlier.
When it came time for each to speak in public
And weave a spell of wisdom with their words,
Menelaus spoke fluently enough, to the point
And very clearly, but briefly, since he is not               *230*

A man of many words. Being older, he spoke first.
Then Odysseus, the master strategist, rose quickly,
But just stood there, his eyes fixed on the ground.
He did not move his staff forward or backward
But held it steady. You would have thought him          *235*
A dull, surly lout without any wit. But when he
Opened his mouth and projected his voice
The words fell down like snowflakes in a blizzard.
No mortal could have vied with Odysseus then,
And we no longer held his looks against him."           *240*

The third hero old Priam saw was Ajax.

"And who is that giant of a Greek over there,
Head and shoulders above the other Achaeans?"

And Helen, shining in her long trailing robes:

"That is big Ajax, the army's mountain.                 *245*
Standing beyond him is Idomeneus,
Like a god, with his Cretan commanders.
He used to come often from Crete
And Menelaus would entertain him
In our house. And now I can make out                    *250*
All the other Greeks, those I know
And whose names I could tell you.
But there are two commanders I do not see,
Castor the horsebreaker and the boxer
Polydeuces, my brothers, born of one mother.            *255*
Either they didn't come here from lovely Lacedaemon,
Or else they did come in their seagoing ships
But avoid the company of the fighting men
In horror of the shame and disgrace that are mine."

But they had long been held by the life-giving earth    *260*
There in Lacedaemon, their ancestral land.

  And now the heralds came up to the town
With the sacrificial victims, the two rams,

And as fruit of the fields, hearty wine
In a goatskin bag. The herald Idaeus                          265
Held a gleaming bowl and a golden chalice
And roused the old man with this speech:

"Rise, son of Laomedon.
The best men of Troy and Achaea summon you
Down to the plain to swear solemn oaths.                     270
Paris and Menelaus will fight
A duel for the woman, and she will
Follow the winner with all her possessions.
Everyone else will swear oaths of friendship,
We to live here in the fertile Troad,                        275
And they to go back to bluegrass Argos
And Achaea with its beautiful women."

The old man stiffened.
He ordered his companions to yoke his horses,
Then mounted himself and took the reins.                     280
Antenor rode with him in the beautiful chariot
And they drove out through the Western Gate
And onto the plain. They pulled up in the space
Between the two armies and stepped down to the earth.

Agamemnon rose,                                              285
And Odysseus, deep in thought.

Heralds brought the animals for the oaths
And mixed wine in the great bowl.
They poured water over the kings' hands,
Then Agamemnon drew the knife                                290
That hung by his sword scabbard
And cut hairs from the rams' heads.
The heralds gave these to the leaders on both sides,
And Agamemnon lifted his palms to the sky:

"Zeus, Father, Lord of Ida,                                  295
Greatest and most glorious;
Helios, who sees all and hears all;

Rivers and Earth, and Powers below
Who punish perjurers after death,
Witness and protect these sacred Oaths:                    *300*
If Paris Alexander kills Menelaus,
Helen and all her goods are his,
And we will sail away in our ships.
But if Menelaus kills Paris,
The Trojans will surrender Helen                           *305*
With all her goods and pay the Argives
A fit penalty for generations to come.
If Priam and Priam's sons refuse,
Upon Paris' death, this penalty to me,
I swear to wage this war to its end."                      *310*

He spoke, then slashed the rams' throats
And put the gasping animals on the ground,
Their proud temper undone by whetted bronze.

Then they all filled their cups
With wine from the bowl and poured libations               *315*
To the gods eternal and prayed,
Greek and Trojan alike, in words like these:

"Zeus almighty and most glorious
And all you other immortal gods,
Whoever breaks this oath and truce,                        *320*
May their brains spill to the ground
Like this wine, theirs and their children's,
And may other men master their wives."

But Zeus would not fulfill their prayers.

Then Priam spoke his mind:                                 *325*

"Hear me, Trojans and Achaean soldiers:
I am going back now to windswept Ilion
Since I cannot bear to see with my own eyes
My dear son fighting with Menelaus,
Who is dear to Ares. Zeus and the other immortals          *330*

Doubtless know whose death is destined."

And this man who was a god's equal
Loaded the rams onto his chariot
For interment in Trojan soil, mounted,
And took the reins. Antenor stood behind him          *335*
And together they drove back to Ilion.

Priam's son Hector and brilliant Odysseus
First measured off an arena and then
Shook lots in a bronze helmet to decide
Which of the two would cast his spear first.          *340*
You could see hands lifted to heaven
On both sides and hear whispered prayers:

"Death, Lord Zeus,
For whichever of the two
Started this business,          *345*
But grant us your peace."

Great Hector shook the helmet, sunlight
Glancing off his own as he looked away,
And out jumped Paris' lot.

                         The armies          *350*
Sat down, rank after rank, tooled weapons
And high-stepping horses idle by each man.

The heroes armed.

Paris, silken-haired Helen's present husband,
Bound greaves on his shins with silver clasps,          *355*
Put on his brother Lycaon's breastplate,
Which fit him well, slung around his shoulders
A bronze sword inlaid with silver
And a large, heavy shield. On his head he placed
A crested helmet, and the horsehair plume          *360*
Nodded menacingly.

Likewise Menelaus' gear.
They put their armor on in the ranks
And then stepped out into no-man's-land,
A cold light in their eyes.                                      *365*

Veterans on both sides, horse-breaking Trojans
And bronze-kneed Greeks, just sat and stared.
They stood close, closer, in the measured arena,
Shaking their spears, half-mad with jealousy.
And then Paris threw. A long shadow trailed his spear      *370*
As it moved through the air, and it hit the circle
Of Menelaus' shield, but the spearpoint crumpled
Against its tough metal skin. It was Menelaus' turn now,
And as he rose in his bronze he prayed to Zeus:

"Lord Zeus, make Paris pay for the evil he's done to me,      *375*
Smite him down with my hands so that men for all time
Will fear to transgress against a host's offered friendship."

With this prayer behind it Menelaus' spear
Carried through Paris' polished shield
And bored into the intricate breastplate,                   *380*
The point shearing his shirt and nicking his ribs
As Paris twisted aside from black fatality.
Menelaus drew his silver-hammered sword
And came down with it hard on the crest
Of Paris' helmet, but the blade shattered                   *385*
Into three or four pieces and fell from his hands.
Menelaus groaned and looked up to the sky:

"Father Zeus, no god curses us more than you.
I thought Paris was going to pay for his crimes,
And now my sword has broken in my hands,                    *390*
And my spear's thrown away. I missed the bastard!"

As Menelaus spoke he lunged forward
And twisted his fingers into the thick horsehair
On Paris' helmet, pivoted on his heel,
And started dragging him back to the Greeks.                *395*

The tooled-leather chinstrap of Paris' helmet
Was cutting into his neck's tender skin,
And Menelaus would have dragged him
All the way back and won no end of glory.
But Aphrodite, Zeus' daughter, had all this                    400
In sharp focus and snapped the oxhide chinstrap,
Leaving Menelaus clenching an empty helmet,
Which the hero, spinning like a discus thrower,
Heaved into the hands of the Greek spectators.
Then he went back for the kill.                               405
                        But Aphrodite
Whisked Paris away with the sleight of a goddess,
Enveloping him in mist, and lofted him into
The incensed air of his vaulted bedroom.
Then she went for Helen, and found her                        410
In a crowd of Trojan women high on the tower.

A withered hand tugged at Helen's fragrant robe.

The goddess was now the phantom of an old woman
Who had spun wool for Helen back in Lacedaemon,
Beautiful wool, and Helen loved her dearly.                   415
In this crone's guise Aphrodite spoke to Helen:

"Over here. Paris wants you to come home.
He's propped up on pillows in your bedroom,
So silky and beautiful you'd never think
He'd just come from combat, but was going to a dance,         420
Or coming from a dance and had just now sat down."

This wrung Helen's heart. She knew
It was the goddess—the beautiful neck,
The irresistible line of her breasts,
The iridescent eyes. She was in awe                           425
For a moment, and then spoke to her:

"You eerie thing, why do you love
Lying to me like this? Where are you taking me now?
Phrygia? Beautiful Maeonia? Another city

Where you have some other boyfriend for me?　　　430
Or is it because Menelaus, having just beaten Paris,
Wants to take his hateful wife back to his house
That you stand here now with treachery in your heart?
Go sit by Paris yourself! Descend from the gods' high road,
Allow your precious feet not to tread on Olympus,　　　435
Go fret over him constantly, protect him.
Maybe someday he'll make you his wife—or even his slave.
I'm not going back there. It would be treason
To share his bed. The Trojan women
Would hold me at fault. I have enough pain as it is."　　　440

And Aphrodite, angry with her, said:

"Don't vex me, bitch, or I may let go of you
And hate you as extravagantly as I love you now.
I can make you repulsive to both sides, you know,
Trojans and Greeks, and then where will you be?"　　　445

Helen was afraid, and this child of Zeus
Pulled her silvery-white linens around her
And walked silently through the Trojan women,
Eluding them completely. The goddess went ahead
And led her to Paris' beautiful house. The servants　　　450
Suddenly all found something to do.
Helen moved like daylight to the vaulted bedroom,
Where Aphrodite, smiling, placed a chair for her
Opposite Paris. Helen, daughter of Zeus,
Sat down and, averting her eyes, said reproachfully:　　　455

"Back from the war? You should have died out there,
Beaten by a real hero, my former husband.
You used to boast you were better than Menelaus,
When it came to spear work and hand-to-hand combat.
Why don't you go challenge him to fight again,　　　460
Right now? I wouldn't recommend it, though,
A fair fight between you and Ares' redhead darling.
You'd go down in no time under his spear."

Paris answered her:

                    "Don't insult me, Helen.                        *465*
Menelaus beat me this time—with Athena's help.
Next time I'll beat him. We have gods on our side too.
Enough of this.
                Let's go to bed now and make love.
I've never wanted you so much,                        *470*
Not even when I first took you away
From Lacedaemon in my sailing ship
And made love to you on the island of Cranae.
I want you even more now than I wanted you then."

He walked to the bed, and Helen followed.                        *475*

While the two of them slept in their bed,
Menelaus prowled the ranks looking for Paris.
The Trojan troops, as much as they would have liked to,
Could not produce him. To a man,
They hated Paris as they hated death itself.                        *480*
So Agamemenon, as commander-in-chief, proclaimed:

"Hear me, Trojans, allied troops, and Dardanians:
The victory clearly belongs to Menelaus.
Surrender therefore Argive Helen
And all the possessions that come with her.                        *485*
We will further assess a suitable penalty,
A tribute to be paid for generations to come."

Thus Agamemnon. And the Greeks cheered.

*[Books 4 and 5 are omitted. The truce is broken when the Trojan Pandarus,
at Athena's urging, shoots an arrow into the Greek ranks and wounds
Menelaus. Battle is joined, and the Greeks, led by Diomedes, who wounds
even Aphrodite and Ares, push the Trojans back.]*

# ILIAD 6

The battle was left to rage on the level expanse
Between Troy's two rivers. Bronze spearheads
Drove past each other as the Greek and Trojan armies
Spread like a hemorrhage across the plain.

*[Lines 5–102 are omitted. The Greeks counterattack. The Trojan seer Hele-
nus, Hector's brother, persuades him to return to Troy and ask the women
to pray to Athena.]*

Hector took his brother's advice.
He jumped down from his chariot with his gear
And toured the ranks, a spear in each hand.                    105
He urged them on, and with a trembling roar
The Trojans turned to face the Achaeans.
The Greeks pulled back. It looked to them
As if some god had come from the starry sky
To help the Trojans. It had been a sudden rally.               110
Hector shouted and called to the Trojans:

"Soldiers of Troy, and illustrious allies,
Remember to fight like the men that you are,
While I go to the city and ask the elders
Who sit in council, and our wives, to pray                     115
To the gods and promise bulls by the hundred."

And Hector left, helmet collecting light
Above the black-hide shield whose rim tapped
His ankles and neck with each step he took.

Then Glaucus, son of Hippolochus,                              120
Met Diomedes in no-man's-land.
Both were eager to fight, but first Tydeus' son
Made his voice heard above the battle noise:

"And which mortal hero are you? I've never seen you
Out here before on the fields of glory,                          *125*
And now here you are ahead of everyone,
Ready to face my spear. Pretty bold.
I feel sorry for your parents. Of course,
You may be an immortal, down from heaven.
Far be it from me to fight an immortal god.                      *130*
Not even mighty Lycurgus lived long
After he tangled with the immortals,
Driving the nurses of Dionysus
Down over the Mountain of Nysa
And making them drop their wands                                 *135*
As he beat them with an ox-goad. Dionysus
Was terrified and plunged into the sea,
Where Thetis received him into her bosom,
Trembling with fear at the human's threats.
Then the gods, who live easy, grew angry                         *140*
With Lycurgus, and the Son of Cronus
Made him go blind, and he did not live long,
Hated as he was by the immortal gods.
No, I wouldn't want to fight an immortal.
But if you are human, and shed blood,                            *145*
Step right up for a quick end to your life."

And Glaucus, Hippolochus' son:

"Great son of Tydeus, why ask about my lineage?
Human generations are like leaves in their seasons.
The wind blows them to the ground, but the tree             *150*
Sprouts new ones when spring comes again.
Men too. Their generations come and go.
But if you really do want to hear my story,
You're welcome to listen. Many men know it.
    Ephyra, in the heart of Argive horse country,           *155*
Was home to Sisyphus, the shrewdest man alive,
Sisyphus son of Aeolus. He had a son, Glaucus,
Who was the father of faultless Bellerophon,
A man of grace and courage by gift of the gods.
But Proetus, whom Zeus had made king of Argos,             *160*

Came to hate Bellerophon
And drove him out. It happened this way.
Proetus' wife, the beautiful Anteia,
Was madly in love with Bellerophon
And wanted to have him in her bed.                    *165*
But she couldn't persuade him, not at all,
Because he was so virtuous and wise.
So she made up lies and spoke to the king:
'Either die yourself, Proetus, or kill Bellerophon.
He wanted to sleep with me against my will.'          *170*
The king was furious when he heard her say this.
He did not kill him—he had scruples about that—
But he sent him to Lycia with a folding tablet
On which he had scratched many evil signs,
And told him to give it to Anteia's father,           *175*
To get him killed. So off he went to Lycia,
With an immortal escort, and when he reached
The river Xanthus, the king there welcomed him
And honored him with entertainment
For nine solid days, killing an ox each day.          *180*
But when the tenth dawn spread her rosy light,
He questioned him and asked to see the tokens
He brought from Proetus, his daughter's husband.
And when he saw the evil tokens from Proetus,
He ordered him, first, to kill the Chimaera,          *185*
A raging monster, divine, inhuman—
A lion in the front, a serpent in the rear,
In the middle a goat—and breathing fire.
Bellerophon killed her, trusting signs from the gods.
Next he had to fight the glorious Solymi,             *190*
The hardest battle, he said, he ever fought,
And, third, the Amazons, women the peers of men.
As he journeyed back the king wove another wile.
He chose the best men in all wide Lycia
And laid an ambush. Not one returned home;            *195*
Blameless Bellerophon killed them all.
When the king realized his guest had divine blood,
He kept him there and gave him his daughter
And half of all his royal honor. Moreover,

The Lycians cut out for him a superb                                200
Tract of land, plow-land and orchard.
His wife, the princess, bore him three children,
Isander, Hippolochus, and Laodameia.
Zeus in his wisdom slept with Laodameia,
And she bore him the godlike warrior Sarpedon.                      205
But even Bellerophon lost the gods' favor
And went wandering alone over the Aleian plain.
His son Isander was slain by Ares
As he fought against the glorious Solymi,
And his daughter was killed by Artemis                             210
Of the golden reins. But Hippolochus
Bore me, and I am proud he is my father.
He sent me to Troy with strict instructions
To be the best ever, better than all the rest,
And not to bring shame on the race of my fathers,                  215
The noblest men in Ephyra and Lycia.
This, I am proud to say, is my lineage."

Diomedes grinned when he heard all this.
He planted his spear in the bounteous earth
And spoke gently to the Lycian prince:                             220

"We have old ties of hospitality!
My grandfather Oeneus long ago
Entertained Bellerophon in his halls
For twenty days, and they gave each other
Gifts of friendship. Oeneus gave                                   225
A belt bright with scarlet, and Bellerophon
A golden cup, which I left at home.
I don't remember my father Tydeus,
Since I was very small when he left for Thebes
In the war that killed so many Achaeans.                           230
But that makes me your friend and you my guest
If ever you come to Argos, as you are my friend
And I your guest whenever I travel to Lycia.
So we can't cross spears with each other
Even in the thick of battle. There are enough                      235
Trojans and allies for me to kill, whomever

A god gives me and I can run down myself.
And enough Greeks for you to kill as you can.
And let's exchange armor, so everyone will know
That we are friends from our fathers' days."                    240

With this said, they vaulted from their chariots,
Clasped hands, and pledged their friendship.
But Zeus took away Glaucus' good sense,
For he exchanged his golden armor for bronze,
The worth of one hundred oxen for nine.                          245

 When Hector reached the oak tree by the Western Gate,
Trojan wives and daughters ran up to him,
Asking about their children, their brothers,
Their kinsmen, their husbands. He told them all,
Each woman in turn, to pray to the gods.                         250
Sorrow clung to their heads like mist.
Then he came to Priam's palace, a beautiful
Building made of polished stone with a central courtyard
Flanked by porticoes, upon which opened fifty
Adjoining rooms, where Priam's sons                              255
Slept with their wives. Across the court
A suite of twelve more bedrooms housed
His modest daughters and their husbands.
It was here that Hector's mother met him,
A gracious woman, with Laodice,                                  260
Her most beautiful daughter, in tow.
Hecuba took his hand in hers and said:

"Hector, my son, why have you left the war
And come here? Are those abominable Greeks
Wearing you down in the fighting outside,                        265
And does your heart lead you to our acropolis
To stretch your hands upward to Zeus?
But stay here while I get you
Some honey-sweet wine, so you can pour a libation
To Father Zeus first and the other immortals,                   270
Then enjoy some yourself, if you will drink.
Wine greatly bolsters a weary man's spirits,

And you are weary from defending your kinsmen."

Sunlight shimmered on great Hector's helmet.

"Mother, don't offer me any wine.                                    *275*
It would drain the power out of my limbs.
I have too much reverence to pour a libation
With unwashed hands to Zeus almighty,
Or to pray to Cronion in the black cloudbanks
Spattered with blood and the filth of battle.                       *280*
But you must go to the War Goddess' temple
To make sacrifice with a band of old women.
Choose the largest and loveliest robe in the house,
The one that is dearest of all to you,
And place it on the knees of braided Athena.                        *285*
And promise twelve heifers to her in her temple,
Unblemished yearlings, if she will pity
The town of Troy, its wives, and its children,
And if she will keep from holy Ilion
Wild Diomedes, who's raging with his spear.                         *290*
Go then to the temple of Athena the War Goddess,
And I will go over to summon Paris,
If he will listen to what I have to say.
I wish the earth would gape open beneath him.
Olympian Zeus has bred him as a curse                               *295*
To Troy, to Priam, and all Priam's children.
If I could see him dead and gone to Hades,
I think my heart might be eased of its sorrow."

Thus Hector. Hecuba went to the great hall
And called to her handmaidens, and they                             *300*
Gathered together the city's old women.
She went herself to a fragrant storeroom
Which held her robes, the exquisite work
Of Sidonian women whom godlike Paris
Brought from Phoenicia when he sailed the sea                       *305*
On the voyage he made for high-born Helen.
Hecuba chose the robe that lay at the bottom,
The most beautiful of all, woven of starlight,

And bore it away as a gift for Athena.
A stream of old women followed behind.                          *310*

They came to the temple of Pallas Athena
On the city's high rock, and the doors were opened
By fair-cheeked Theano, daughter of Cisseus
And wife of Antenor, breaker of horses.

The Trojans had made her Athena's priestess.                    *315*
With ritual cries they all lifted their hands
To Pallas Athena. Theano took the robe
And laid it on the knees of the rich-haired goddess,
Then prayed in supplication to Zeus' daughter:

"Lady Athena who defends our city,                              *320*
Brightest of goddesses, hear our prayer.
Break now the spear of Diomedes
And grant that he fall before the Western Gate,
That we may now offer twelve heifers in this temple,
Unblemished yearlings. Only do thou pity                        *325*
The town of Troy, its wives and its children."

But Pallas Athena denied her prayer.

While they prayed to great Zeus' daughter,
Hector came to Paris' beautiful house,
Which he had built himself with the aid                         *330*
Of the best craftsmen in all wide Troy:
Sleeping quarters, a hall, and a central courtyard
Near to Priam's and Hector's on the city's high rock.
Hector entered, Zeus' light upon him,
A spear sixteen feet long cradled in his hand,                  *335*
The bronze point gleaming, and the ferrule gold.
He found Paris in the bedroom, busy with his weapons,
Fondling his curved bow, his fine shield, and breastplate.
Helen of Argos sat with her household women
Directing their exquisite handicraft.                           *340*

Hector meant to shame Paris and provoke him:

"This is a fine time to be nursing your anger,
You idiot! We're dying out there defending the walls.
It's because of you the city is in this hellish war.
If you saw someone else holding back from combat          345
You'd pick a fight with him yourself. Now get up
Before the whole city goes up in flames!"

And Paris, handsome as a god:

"That's no more than just, Hector,
But listen now to what I have to say.                     350
It's not out of anger or spite toward the Trojans
I've been here in my room. I only wanted
To recover from my pain. My wife was just now
Encouraging me to get up and fight,
And that seems the better thing to do.                    355
Victory takes turns with men. Wait for me
While I put on my armor, or go on ahead—
I'm pretty sure I'll catch up with you."

To which Hector said nothing.

But Helen said to him softly:                             360

                        "Brother-in-law
Of a scheming, cold-blooded bitch,
I wish that on the day my mother bore me
A windstorm had swept me away to a mountain
Or into the waves of the restless sea,                    365
Swept me away before all this could happen.
But since the gods have ordained these evils,
Why couldn't I be the wife of a better man,
One sensitive at least to repeated reproaches?
Paris has never had an ounce of good sense                370
And never will. He'll pay for it someday.
But come inside and sit down on this chair,
Dear brother-in-law. You bear such a burden
For my wanton ways and Paris' witlessness.
Zeus has placed this evil fate on us so that              375

In time to come poets will sing of us."

And Hector, in his burnished helmet:

"Don't ask me to sit, Helen, even though
You love me. You will never persuade me.
My heart is out there with our fighting men.          *380*
They already feel my absence from battle.
Just get Paris moving, and have him hurry
So he can catch up with me while I'm still
Inside the city. I'm going to my house now
To see my family, my wife and my boy. I don't know          *385*
Whether I'll ever be back to see them again, or if
The gods will destroy me at the hands of the Greeks."

And Hector turned and left. He came to his house
But did not find white-armed Andromache there.
She had taken the child and a robed attendant          *390*
And stood on the tower, lamenting and weeping—
His blameless wife. When Hector didn't find her inside,
He paused on his way out and called to the servants:

"Can any of you women tell me exactly
Where Andromache went when she left the house?          *395*
To one of my sisters or one of my brothers' wives?
Or to the temple of Athena along with the other
Trojan women to beseech the dread goddess?"

The spry old housekeeper answered him:

"Hector, if you want the exact truth, she didn't go          *400*
To any of your sisters, or any of your brothers' wives,
Or to the temple of Athena along with the other
Trojan women to beseech the dread goddess.
She went to Ilion's great tower, because she heard
The Trojans were pressed and the Greeks were strong.          *405*
She ran off to the wall like a madwoman,
And the nurse went with her, carrying the child."

Thus the housekeeper, but Hector was gone,
Retracing his steps through the stone and tile streets
Of the great city, until he came to the Western Gate.                  *410*
He was passing through it out onto the plain
When his wife came running up to meet him,
His beautiful wife, Andromache,
A gracious woman, daughter of great Eëtion,
Eëtion, who lived in the forests of Plakos                              *415*
And ruled the Cilicians from Thebes-under-Plakos—
His daughter was wed to bronze-helmeted Hector.
She came up to him now, and the nurse with her
Held to her bosom their baby boy,
Hector's beloved son, beautiful as starlight,                          *420*
Whom Hector had named Scamandrius
But everyone else called Astyanax, Lord of the City,
For Hector alone could save Ilion now.
He looked at his son and smiled in silence.
Andromache stood close to him, shedding tears,                         *425*
Clinging to his arm as she spoke these words:

"Possessed is what you are, Hector. Your courage
Is going to kill you, and you have no feeling left
For your little boy or for me, the luckless woman
Who will soon be your widow. It won't be long                          *430*
Before the whole Greek army swarms and kills you.
And when they do, it will be better for me
To sink into the earth. When I lose you, Hector,
There will be nothing left, no one to turn to,
Only pain. My father and mother are dead.                              *435*
Achilles killed my father when he destroyed
Our city, Thebes with its high gates,
But had too much respect to despoil his body.
He burned it instead with all his armor
And heaped up a barrow. And the spirit women                           *440*
Came down from the mountain, daughters
Of the storm god, and planted elm trees around it.
I had seven brothers once in that great house.
All seven went down to Hades on a single day,
Cut down by Achilles in one blinding sprint                            *445*

Through their shambling cattle and silver sheep.
Mother, who was queen in the forests of Plakos,
He took back as prisoner, with all her possessions,
Then released her for a fortune in ransom.
She died in our house, shot by Artemis' arrows.          *450*
Hector, you are my father, you are my mother,
You are my brother and my blossoming husband.
But show some pity and stay here by the tower,
Don't make your child an orphan, your wife a widow.
Station your men here by the fig tree, where the city     *455*
Is weakest because the wall can be scaled.
Three times their elite have tried an attack here
Rallying around Ajax or glorious Idomeneus
Or Atreus' sons or mighty Diomedes,
Whether someone in on the prophecy told them              *460*
Or they are driven here by something in their heart."

And great Hector, helmet shining, answered her:

"Yes, Andromache, I worry about all this myself,
But my shame before the Trojans and their wives,
With their long robes trailing, would be too terrible     *465*
If I hung back from battle like a coward.
And my heart won't let me. I have learned to be
One of the best, to fight in Troy's first ranks,
Defending my father's honor and my own.
Deep in my heart I know too well                          *470*
There will come a day when holy Ilion will perish,
And Priam and the people under Priam's ash spear.
But the pain I will feel for the Trojans then,
For Hecuba herself and for Priam king,
For my many fine brothers who will have by then           *475*
Fallen in the dust behind enemy lines—
All that pain is nothing to what I will feel
For you, when some bronze-armored Greek
Leads you away in tears, on your first day of slavery.
And you will work some other woman's loom                 *480*
In Argos or carry water from a Spartan spring,
All against your will, under great duress.

And someone, seeing you crying, will say,
'That is the wife of Hector, the best of all
The Trojans when they fought around Ilion.'                    485
Someday someone will say that, renewing your pain
At having lost such a man to fight off the day
Of your enslavement. But may I be dead
And the earth heaped up above me
Before I hear your cry as you are dragged away."              490

With these words, resplendent Hector
Reached for his child, who shrank back screaming
Into his nurse's bosom, terrified of his father's
Bronze-encased face and the horsehair plume
He saw nodding down from the helmet's crest.                  495
This forced a laugh from his father and mother,
And Hector removed the helmet from his head
And set it on the ground all shimmering with light.
Then he kissed his dear son and swung him up gently
And said a prayer to Zeus and the other immortals:           500

"Zeus and all gods: grant that this my son
Become, as I am, foremost among Trojans,
Brave and strong, and ruling Ilion with might.
And may men say he is far better than his father
When he returns from war, bearing bloody spoils,             505
Having killed his man. And may his mother rejoice."

And he put his son in the arms of his wife,
And she enfolded him in her fragrant bosom
Laughing through her tears. Hector pitied her
And stroked her with his hand and said to her:               510

"You worry too much about me, Andromache.
No one is going to send me to Hades before my time,
And no man has ever escaped his fate, rich or poor,
Coward or hero, once born into this world.
Go back to the house now and take care of your work,         515
The loom and the shuttle, and tell the servants
To get on with their jobs. War is the work of men,

Of all the Trojan men, and mine especially."

With these words, Hector picked up
His plumed helmet, and his wife went back home,                    520
Turning around often, her cheeks flowered with tears.
When she came to the house of man-slaying Hector,
She found a throng of servants inside,
And raised among these women the ritual lament.
And so they mourned for Hector in his house                        525
Although he was still alive, for they did not think
He would ever again come back from the war,
Or escape the murderous hands of the Greeks.

   Paris meanwhile
                    Did not dally long in his high halls.          530
He put on his magnificent bronze-inlaid gear
And sprinted with assurance out through the city.

   *Picture a horse that has fed on barley in his stall*
   *Breaking his halter and galloping across the plain,*
   *Making for his accustomed swim in the river,*          535
   *A glorious animal, head held high, mane streaming*
   *Like wind on his shoulders. Sure of his splendor*
   *He prances by the horse-runs and the mares in pasture.*

That was how Paris, son of Priam, came down
From the high rock of Pergamum,                                     540
Gleaming like amber and laughing in his armor,
And his feet were fast.
                  He caught up quickly
With Hector just as he turned from the spot
Where he'd talked with his wife, and called out:                   545

"Well, dear brother, have I delayed you too much?
Am I not here in time, just as you asked?"

Hector turned, his helmet flashing light:

"I don't understand you, Paris.

No one could slight your work in battle.                                              *550*
You're a strong fighter, but you slack off–
You don't have the will. It breaks my heart
To hear what the Trojans say about you.
It's on your account they have all this trouble.
Come on, let's go. We can settle this later,                                           *555*
If Zeus ever allows us to offer in our halls
The wine bowl of freedom to the gods above,
After we drive these bronze-kneed Greeks from Troy."


*[Books 7 and 8 are omitted. Hector and Paris return to battle. Hector offers
to fight a duel with any Greek. Ajax responds to the challenge, and the two
fight to a draw. The Greeks and Trojans agree to a truce so that they can
bury the dead. The Greeks build a wall and a trench around their camp.
Zeus orders the other gods not to intervene, and with his support the Tro-
jans gain the advantage.]*


# ILIAD 9


*[Lines 1–185 are omitted. Agamemnon sends Odysseus, Phoenix, and Ajax
to apologize to Achilles on his behalf and to ask him to return to battle.]*


   They went in tandem along the seething shore,
Praying over and over to the god in the surf
For an easy time in convincing Achilles.
They came to the Myrmidons' ships and huts
And found him plucking clear notes on a lyre—                                          *190*
A beautiful instrument with a silver bridge
He had taken when he ransacked Eëtion's town—
Accompanying himself as he sang the glories
Of heroes in war. He was alone with Patroclus,
Who sat in silence waiting for him to finish.                                          *195*
His visitors came forward, Odysseus first,

And stood before him. Surprised, Achilles
Rose from his chair still holding his lyre.
Patroclus, when he saw them, also rose,
And Achilles, swift and sure, received them:                    *200*

"Welcome. Things must be bad to bring you here,
The Greeks I love best, even in my rage."

With these words Achilles led them in
And had them sit on couches and rugs
Dyed purple, and he called to Patroclus:                        *205*

"A larger bowl, son of Menoetius,
And stronger wine, and cups all around.
My dearest friends are beneath my roof."

Patroclus obliged his beloved companion.
Then he cast a carving block down in the firelight              *210*
And set on it a sheep's back and a goat's,
And a hog chine too, marbled with fat.
Automedon held the meat while Achilles
Carved it carefully and spitted the pieces.
Patroclus, godlike in the fire's glare,                         *215*
Fed the blaze. When the flames died down
He laid the spits over the scattered embers,
Resting them on stones, and sprinkled the morsels
With holy salt. When the meat was roasted
He laid it on platters and set out bread                        *220*
In exquisite baskets. Achilles served the meat,
Then sat down by the wall opposite Odysseus
And asked Patroclus to offer sacrifice.
After he threw the offerings in the fire,
They helped themselves to the meal before them,                 *225*
And when they had enough of food and drink,
Ajax nodded to Phoenix. Odysseus saw this,
And filling a cup he lifted it to Achilles:

"To your health, Achilles, for a generous feast.
There is no shortage in Agamemnon's hut,                        *230*

Or now here in yours, of satisfying food.
But the pleasures of the table are not on our minds.
We fear the worst. It is doubtful
That we can save the ships without your strength.
The Trojans and their allies are encamped                                235
Close to the wall that surrounds our black ships
And are betting that we can't keep them
From breaking through. They may be right.
Zeus has been encouraging them with signs,
Lightning on the right. Hector trusts this—                              240
And his own strength—and has been raging
Recklessly, like a man possessed.
He is praying for dawn to come early
So he can fulfill his threat to lop the horns
From the ships' sterns, burn the hulls to ash,                           245
And slaughter the Achaeans dazed in the smoke.
This is my great fear, that the gods make good
Hector's threats, dooming us to die in Troy
Far from the fields of home. Up with you, then,
If you intend at all, even at this late hour,                            250
To save our army from these howling Trojans.
Think of yourself, of the regret you will feel
For harm that will prove irreparable.
This is the last chance to save your countrymen.
Is it not true, my friend, that your father Peleus                       255
Told you as he sent you off with Agamemnon:
'My son, as for strength, Hera and Athena
Will bless you if they wish, but it is up to you
To control your proud spirit. A friendly heart
Is far better. Steer clear of scheming strife,                           260
So that Greeks young and old will honor you.'
You have forgotten what the old man said,
But you can still let go of your anger, right now.
Agamemnon is offering you worthy gifts
If you will give up your grudge. Hear me                                 265
While I list the gifts he proposed in his hut:
Seven unfired tripods, ten gold bars,
Twenty burnished cauldrons, a dozen horses—
Solid, prizewinning racehorses

Who have won him a small fortune—                                        *270*
And seven women who do impeccable work,
Surpassingly beautiful women from Lesbos
He chose for himself when you captured the town.
And with them will be the woman he took from you,
Briseus' daughter, and he will solemnly swear                            *275*
He never went to her bed and lay with her
Or did what is natural between women and men.
All this you may have at once. And if it happens
That the gods allow us to sack Priam's city,
You may when the Greeks are dividing the spoils                          *280*
Load a ship to the brim with gold and bronze,
And choose for yourself the twenty Trojan women
Who are next in beauty to Argive Helen.
And if we return to the rich land of Argos,
You would marry his daughter, and he would honor you                     *285*
As he does Orestes, who is being reared in luxury.
He has three daughters in his fortress palace,
Chrysothemis, Laodice, and Iphianassa.
You may lead whichever you like as your bride
Back to Peleus' house, without paying anything,                          *290*
And he would give her a dowry richer than any
A father has ever given his daughter.
And he will give you seven populous cities,
Cardamyle, Enope, grassy Hire,
Sacred Pherae, Antheia with its meadowlands,                             *295*
Beautiful Aepeia, and Pedasus, wine country.
They are all near the sea, on sandy Pylos' frontier,
And cattlemen live there, rich in herds and flocks,
Who will pay you tribute as if you were a god
And fulfill the shining decrees of your scepter.                         *300*
All this he will do if you give up your grudge.
But if Agamemnon is too hateful to you,
Himself and his gifts, think of all the others
Suffering up and down the line, and of the glory
You will win from them. They will honor you                              *305*
Like a god.
              And don't forget Hector.
You just might get him now. He's coming in close,

Deluded into thinking that he has no match
In the Greek army that has landed on his beach."                    *310*

And Achilles, strong, swift, and godlike:

"Son of Laertes in the line of Zeus,
Odysseus the strategist—I can see
That I have no choice but to speak my mind
And tell you exactly how things are going to be.                    *315*
Either that or sit through endless sessions
Of people whining at me. I hate it like I hate hell
The man who says one thing and thinks another.
So this is how I see it.
I cannot imagine Agamemnon,                    *320*
Or any other Greek, persuading me,
Not after the thanks I got for fighting this war,
Going up against the enemy day after day.
It doesn't matter if you stay in camp or fight—
In the end, everybody comes out the same.                    *325*
Coward and hero get the same reward:
You die whether you slack off or work.
And what do I have for all my suffering,
Constantly putting my life on the line?
Like a bird who feeds her chicks                    *330*
Whatever she finds, and goes without herself,
That's what I've been like, lying awake
Through sleepless nights, in battle for days
Soaked in blood, fighting men for their wives.
I've raided twelve cities with our ships                    *335*
And eleven on foot in the fertile Troad,
Looted them all, brought back heirlooms
By the ton, and handed it all over
To Atreus' son, who hung back in camp
Raking it in and distributing damn little.                    *340*
What the others did get they at least got to keep.
They all have their prizes, everyone but me—
I'm the only Greek from whom he took something back.
He should be happy with the woman he has.
Why do the Greeks have to fight the Trojans?                    *345*

Why did Agamemnon lead the army to Troy
If not for the sake of fair-haired Helen?
Do you have to be descended from Atreus
To love your mate? Every decent, sane man
Loves his woman and cares for her, as I did,                    350
Loved her from my heart. It doesn't matter
That I won her with my spear. He took her,
Took her right out of my hands, cheated me,
And now he thinks he's going to win me back?
He can forget it. I know how things stand.                    355
It's up to you, Odysseus, and the other kings
To find a way to keep the fire from the ships.
He's been pretty busy without me, hasn't he,
Building a wall, digging a moat around it,
Pounding in stakes for a palisade.                    360
None of that stuff will hold Hector back.
When I used to fight for the Greeks,
Hector wouldn't come out farther from his wall
Than the oak tree by the Western Gate.
He waited for me there once, and barely escaped.                    365
Now that I don't want to fight him anymore,
I will sacrifice to Zeus and all gods tomorrow,
Load my ships, and launch them on the sea.
Take a look if you want, if you give a damn,
And you'll see my fleet on the Hellespont                    370
In the early light, my men rowing hard.
With good weather from the sea god,
I'll reach Phthia after a three-day sail.
I left a lot behind when I hauled myself here,
And I'll bring back more, gold and bronze,                    375
Silken-waisted women, grey iron—
Everything except the prize of honor
The warlord Agamemnon gave me
And in his insulting arrogance took back.
So report back to him everything I say,                    380
And report it publicly—get the Greeks angry,
In case the shameless bastard still thinks
He can steal us blind. He doesn't dare
Show his dogface here. Fine. I don't want

To have anything to do with him either.                    *385*
He cheated me, wronged me. Never again.
He's had it. He can go to hell in peace,
The half-wit that Zeus has made him.
His gifts? His gifts mean nothing to me.
Not even if he offered me ten or twenty times          *390*
His present gross worth and added to it
All the trade Orchomenus does in a year,
All the wealth laid up in Egyptian Thebes,
The wealthiest city in all the world,
Where they drive two hundred teams of horses          *395*
Out through each of its hundred gates.
Not even if Agamemnon gave me gifts
As numberless as grains of sand or dust,
Would he persuade me or touch my heart—
Not until he's paid in full for all my grief.          *400*
His daughter? I would not marry
The daughter of Agamemnon son of Atreus
If she were as lovely as golden Aphrodite
Or could weave like owl-eyed Athena.
Let him choose some other Achaean                      *405*
More to his lordly taste. If the gods
Preserve me and I get home safe
Peleus will find me a wife himself.
There are many Greek girls in Hellas and Phthia,
Daughters of chieftains who rule the cities.           *410*
I can have my pick of any of them.
I've always wanted to take a wife there,
A woman to have and to hold, someone with whom
I can enjoy all the goods old Peleus has won.
Nothing is worth my life, not all the riches          *415*
They say Troy held before the Greeks came,
Not all the wealth in Phoebus Apollo's
Marble shrine up in craggy Pytho.
Cattle and flocks are there for the taking;
You can always get tripods and chestnut horses.       *420*
But a man's life cannot be won back
Once his breath has passed beyond his clenched teeth.
My mother Thetis, a moving silver grace,

Tells me two fates sweep me on to my death.
If I stay here and fight, I'll never return home,                    *425*
But my glory will be undying forever.
If I return home to my dear fatherland
My glory is lost but my life will be long,
And death that ends all will not catch me soon.
As for the rest of you, I would advise you too                      *430*
To sail back home, since there's no chance now
Of storming Ilion's height. Zeus has stretched
His hand above her, making her people bold.
What's left for you now is to go back to the council
And announce my message. It's up to them                            *435*
To come up with another plan to save the ships
And the army with them, since this one,
Based on appeasing my anger, won't work.
Phoenix can spend the night here. Tomorrow
He sails with me on our voyage home,                                *440*
If he wants to, that is. I won't force him to come."

He spoke, and they were hushed in silence,
Shocked by his speech and his stark refusal.
Finally the old horseman Phoenix spoke,
Bursting into tears. He felt the ships were lost.                   *445*

"If you have set your mind on going home,
Achilles, and will do nothing to save the ships
From being burnt, if your heart is that angry,
How could I stay here without you, my boy,
All by myself? Peleus sent me with you                              *450*
On that day you left Phthia to go to Agamemnon,
A child still, knowing nothing of warfare
Or assemblies where men distinguish themselves.
He sent me to you to teach you this—
To be a speaker of words and a doer of deeds.                       *455*
I could not bear to be left behind now
Apart from you, child, not even if a god
Promised to smooth my wrinkles and make me
As young and strong as I was when I first left
The land of Hellas and its beautiful women.                         *460*

I was running away from a quarrel with Amyntor,
My father, who was angry with me
Over his concubine, a fair-haired woman
Whom he loved as much as he scorned his wife,
My mother. She implored me constantly                        465
To make love to his concubine so that this woman
Would learn to hate the old man. I did as she asked.
My father found out and cursed me roundly,
Calling on the Furies to ensure that never
Would a child of mine sit on his knees.                      470
The gods answered his prayers, Underworld Zeus
And dread Persephone. I decided to kill him
With a sharp sword, but some god calmed me down—
Putting in my mind what people would say,
The names they would call me—so that in fact                 475
I would not be known as a parricide.
From then on I could not bear to linger
In my father's house, although my friends
And my family tried to get me to stay,
Entreating me, slaughtering sheep and cattle,                480
Roasting whole pigs on spits, and drinking
Jar after jar of the old man's wine.
For nine solid days they kept watch on me,
Working in shifts, staying up all night.
The fires stayed lit, one under the portico                  485
Of the main courtyard, one on the porch
In front of my bedroom door. On the tenth night,
When it got dark, I broke through the latches
And vaulted over the courtyard fence,
Eluding the watchmen and servant women.                      490
I was on the run through wide Hellas
And made it to Phthia's black soil, her flocks,
And to Lord Peleus. He welcomed me kindly
And loved me as a father loves his only son,
A grown son who will inherit great wealth.                   495
He made me rich and settled me on the border,
Where I lived as king of the Dolopians.
I made you what you are, my godlike Achilles,
And loved you from my heart. You wouldn't eat,

Whether it was at a feast or a meal in the house, 500
Unless I set you on my lap and cut your food up
And fed it to you and held the wine to your lips.
Many a time you wet the tunic on my chest,
Burping up wine when you were colicky.
I went through a lot for you, because I knew 505
The gods would never let me have a child
Of my own. No, I tried to make you my child,
Achilles, so you would save me from ruin.
But you have to master your proud spirit.
It's not right for you to have a pitiless heart. 510
Even the gods can bend. Superior as they are
In honor, power, and every excellence,
They can be turned aside from wrath
When humans who have transgressed
Supplicate them with incense and prayers, 515
With libations and savor of sacrifice.
Yes, for Prayers are daughters of great Zeus.
Lame and wrinkled and with eyes averted,
They are careful to follow in Folly's footsteps,
But Folly is strong and fleet, and outruns them all, 520
Beating them everywhere and plaguing humans,
Who are cured by the Prayers when they come behind.
Revere the daughters of Zeus when they come,
And they will bless you and hear your cry.
Reject them and refuse them stubbornly, 525
And they will ask Zeus, Cronus' son, to have
Folly plague you, so you will pay in pain.
No, Achilles, grant these daughters of Zeus
The respect that bends all upright men's minds.
If the son of Atreus were not offering gifts 530
And promising more, if he were still raging mad,
I would not ask you to shrug off your grudge
And help the Greeks, no matter how sore their need.
But he is offering gifts and promising more,
And he has sent to you a delegation 535
Of the best men in the army, your dearest friends.
Don't scorn their words or their mission here.
 No one could blame you for being angry before.

We all know stories about heroes of old,
How they were furiously angry, but later on　　　　　540
Were won over with gifts or appeased with words.
I remember a very old story like this, and since
We are all friends here, I will tell it to you now.
　　The Curetes were fighting the Aetolians
In a bloody war around Calydon town.　　　　　　545
The Aetolians were defending their city
And the Curetes meant to burn it down.
This was all because gold-throned Artemis
Had cursed the Curetes, angry that Oeneus
Had not offered her his orchard's first fruits.　　550
The other gods feasted on bulls by the hundred,
But Oeneus forgot somehow or other
Only the sacrifice to great Zeus' daughter.
So the Archer Goddess, angry at heart,
Roused a savage boar, with gleaming white tusks,　　555
And sent him to destroy Oeneus' orchard.
The boar did a good job, uprooting trees
And littering the ground with apples and blossoms.
But Oeneus' son, Meleager, killed it
After getting up a party of hunters and hounds　　560
From many towns: it took more than a few men
To kill this huge boar, and not before
It set many a hunter on the funeral pyre.
But the goddess caused a bitter argument
About the boar's head and shaggy hide　　　　　565
Between the Curetes and Aetolians.
They went to war. While Meleager still fought
The Curetes had the worst of it
And could not remain outside Calydon's wall.
But when wrath swelled Meleager's heart,　　　570
As it swells even the hearts of the wise,
And his anger rose against Althaea his mother,
He lay in bed with his wife, Cleopatra,
Child of Marpessa and the warrior Idas.
Idas once took up his bow against Apollo　　　575
To win lissome Marpessa. Her parents
Called the girl Halcyone back then

Because her mother wept like a halcyon,
The bird of sorrows, because the Archer God,
Phoebus Apollo, had stolen her daughter.                    *580*
Meleager nursed his anger at Cleopatra's side,
Furious because his mother had cursed him,
Cursed him to the gods for murdering his uncle,
Her brother, that is, and she beat the earth,
The nurturing earth, with her hands, and called            *585*
Upon Hades and Persephone the dread,
As she knelt and wet her bosom with tears,
To bring death to her son. And the Fury
Who walks in darkness heard her
From the pit of Erebus, and her heart was iron.            *590*
Soon the enemy was heard at the walls again,
Battering the gates. The Aetolian elders
Sent the city's high priests to pray to Meleager
To come out and defend them, offering him
Fifty acres of Calydon's richest land                      *595*
Wherever he chose, half in vineyard,
Half in clear plow-land, to be cut from the plain.
And the old horseman Oeneus shook his doors,
Standing on the threshold of his gabled room,
And recited a litany of prayers to his son,               *600*
As did his sisters and his queenly mother.
He refused them all, and refused his friends,
His very best friends and boon companions.
No one could move his heart or persuade him
Until the Curetes, having scaled the walls                 *605*
Were burning the city and beating down
His bedroom door. Then his wife wailed
And listed for him all the woes that befall
A captured people—the men killed,
The town itself burnt, the women and children             *610*
Led into slavery. This roused his spirit.
He clapped on armor and went out to fight.
And so he saved the Aetolians from doom
Of his own accord, and they paid him none
Of those lovely gifts, savior or not.                      *615*
    Don't be like that. Don't think that way,

And don't let your spirit turn that way.
The ships will be harder to save when they're burning.
Come while there are gifts, while the Achaeans
Will still honor you as if you were a god.                            620
But if you go into battle without any gifts,
Your honor will be less, save us or not."

And strong, swift-footed Achilles answered:

"I don't need that kind of honor, Phoenix.
My honor comes from Zeus, and I will have it                         625
Among these beaked ships as long as my breath
Still remains and my knees still move.
Now listen to this. You're listening? Good.
Don't try to confuse me with your pleading
On Agamemnon's behalf. If you're his friend                         630
You're no longer mine, although I love you.
Hate him because I hate him. It's as simple as that.
You're like a second father to me. Stay here,
Be king with me and share half the honor.
These others can take my message. Lie down                          635
And spend the night on a soft couch. At daybreak
We will decide whether to set sail or stay."

And he made a silent nod to Patroclus
To spread a thick bed for Phoenix. It was time
For the others to think about leaving. Big Ajax,                     640
Telamon's godlike son, said as much:

"Son of Laertes in the line of Zeus,
Resourceful Odysseus—it's time we go.
I do not think we will accomplish
What we were sent here to do. Our job now                           645
Is to report this news quickly, bad as it is.
They will be waiting to hear. Achilles
Has made his great heart savage.
He is a cruel man, and has no regard
For the love that his friends honored him with,                     650
Beyond anyone else who camps with the ships.

Pitiless. A man accepts compensation
For a murdered brother, a dead son.
The killer goes on living in the same town
After paying blood money, and the bereaved                    *655*
Restrains his proud spirit and broken heart
Because he has received payment. But you,
The gods have replaced your heart
With flint and malice, because of one girl,
One single girl, while we are offering you                    *660*
Seven of the finest women to be found
And many other gifts. Show some generosity
And some respect. We have come under your roof,
We few out of the entire army, trying hard
To be the friends you care for most of all."                  *665*

And Achilles, the great runner, answered him:

"Ajax, son of Telamon in the line of Zeus,
Everything you say is after my own heart.
But I swell with rage when I think of how
The son of Atreus treated me like dirt                        *670*
In public, as if I were some worthless tramp.
Now go, and take back this message:
I won't lift a finger in this bloody war
Until Priam's illustrious son Hector
Comes to the Myrmidons' ships and huts                        *675*
Killing Greeks as he goes and torching the fleet.
But when he comes to my hut and my black ship
I think Hector will stop, for all his battle lust."

He spoke. They poured their libations
And headed for the ships, Odysseus leading.                   *680*
Patroclus ordered a bed made ready
For Phoenix, and the old man lay down
On fleeces and rugs covered with linen
And waited for bright dawn. Achilles slept
In an inner alcove, and by his side                           *685*
Lay a woman he had brought from Lesbos
With high, lovely cheekbones, Diomede her name,

Phorbas' daughter. Patroclus lay down
In the opposite corner, and with him lay Iphis,
A silken girl Achilles had given him                        *690*
When he took steep Scyrus, Enyeus' city.

By now Odysseus and Ajax
Were in Agamemnon's quarters,
Surrounded by officers drinking their health
From gold cups and shouting questions.                      *695*
Agamemnon, the warlord, had priority:

"Odysseus, pride of the Achaeans, tell me,
Is he willing to repel the enemy fire
And save the ships, or does he refuse,
His great heart still in the grip of wrath?"                *700*

Odysseus, who endured all, answered:

"Son of Atreus, most glorious Agamemnon,
Far from quenching his wrath, Achilles
Is filled with even more. He spurns you
And your gifts, and suggests that you                       *705*
Think of a way to save the ships and the army.
He himself threatens, at dawn's first light,
To get his own ships onto the water,
And he said he would advise the others as well
To sail for home, since there is no chance now              *710*
You will storm Ilion's height. Zeus has stretched
His hand above her, making her people bold.
This is what he said, as these men here
Who came with me will tell you, Ajax
And the two heralds, prudent men both.                      *715*
Phoenix will spend the night there. Tomorrow
He sails with Achilles on his voyage home,
If he wants to. He will not be forced to go."

They were stunned by the force of his words
And fell silent for a long time, hushed in grief,           *720*
Until at last Diomedes said in his booming voice:

"Son of Atreus, glorious Agamemnon,
You should never have pleaded with him
Or offered all those gifts. Achilles
Was arrogant enough without your help.          725
Let him do what he wants, stay here
Or get the hell out. He'll fight later, all right,
When he is ready or a god tells him to.
Now I want everyone to do as I say.
Enjoy some food and wine to keep up          730
Your strength, and then get some sleep.
When the rosy light first streaks the sky
Get your troops and horses into formation
Before the ships. Fight in the front yourselves."

The warlords assented, taken aback          735
By the authority of Diomedes' speech.
Each man poured libation and went to his hut,
Where he lay down and took the gift of sleep.


*[Books 10 and 11 are omitted. Odysseus and Diomedes raid the Trojan camp by night. The next day Agamemnon leads the Greeks into battle and distinguishes himself until he is wounded. Then Odysseus and Diomedes are both wounded and withdraw. Nestor suggests to Patroclus that he ask Achilles to allow him to borrow his armor and lead the Myrmidons into battle.]*

# ILIAD 12

*[Lines 1–258 are omitted. Hector leads the Trojans across the trench and
up to the wall around the Greek camp.]*

To the noise of their advance Zeus now added
A wind from Ida's mountains that blew dust                               260
Straight at the ships and the bewildered Greeks.
The sky god was giving the glory to the Trojans
And to Hector.

                Trusting these portents
And their own strength, the Trojans did their best                      265
To breach the wall. Pulling down pickets
And battlements, they threw them to the ground
And set to work prying up the huge beams
The Greeks had used to reinforce the wall.
They were dragging these out, hoping to topple                          270
The entire structure, but even then the Greeks
Refused to give way, patching the battlements
With bullhide and beating off the invaders.

Both Ajaxes were on the wall, patrolling it
And urging on the troops, using harsh words,                            275
Gentle words, whatever it took
To get the men back into the fight:

"Friends!—and I mean everyone from heroes
To camp followers—no one ever said
Men are equal in war. There is work for us all.                         280
You know it yourselves. I don't want a single man
To return to the ships now that you have heard
The rallying cry. Keep the pressure on.
Olympian Zeus may still grant us
To drive the enemy back to the city."                                   285

And they roused the Greeks to battle.

> *Snow flurries fall thick on a winter's day*
> *When Zeus in his cunning rouses himself*
> *To show humans the ammunition he has.*
> *He lulls the winds and he snows and snows*                    290
> *Until he has covered all the mountain tops,*
> *Headlands and meadows and men's plowed fields.*
> *And the snow falls over the harbors*
> *And the shores of the grey sea, and only*
> *The waves keep it off. The rest of the world*                 295
> *Is enveloped in the winter tempest of Zeus.*

The stones flew thick upon the Trojans
And upon the Greeks, and the wooden wall
Was beaten like a drum along its whole length.

For all this, though, Hector and his Trojans                      300
Would never have broken the barred gate
Had not Zeus roused his own son, Sarpedon,
Against the Greeks, as a lion against cattle.
Sarpedon held before him a perfect shield,
Its bronze skin hammered smooth by the smith,                     305
Who had stitched the leather beneath with gold
All around the rim. Holding this shield
And brandishing two spears, Sarpedon advanced.

> *The mountain lion has not fed for days*
> *And is hungry and brave enough to enter*                      310
> *The stone sheep pen and attack the flocks.*
> *Even if he finds herdsmen on the spot*
> *With dogs and spears to protect the fold,*
> *He will not be driven back without a try,*
> *And either he leaps in and seizes a sheep*                    315
> *Or is killed by a spear, as human heroes are.*

Godlike Sarpedon felt impelled
To rush the wall and tear it down.

He turned to Glaucus and said:

"Glaucus, you know how you and I                    *320*
Have the best of everything in Lycia—
Seats, cuts of meat, full cups, everybody
Looking at us as if we were gods?
Not to mention our estates on the Xanthus,
Fine orchards and riverside wheat fields.          *325*
Well, now we have to take our stand at the front,
Where all the best fight, and face the heat of battle,
So that many an armored Lycian will say,
'So they're not inglorious after all,
Our Lycian lords who eat fat sheep                 *330*
And drink the sweetest wine. No,
They're strong, and fight with our best.'
Ah, my friend, if you and I could only
Get out of this war alive and then
Be immortal and ageless all of our days.           *335*
I would never again fight among the foremost
Or send you into battle where men win glory.
But as it is, death is everywhere
In more shapes than we can count,
And since no mortal is immune or can escape,       *340*
Let's go forward, either to give glory
To another man or get glory from him."

Thus Sarpedon. Glaucus nodded, and the two of them
Moved out at the head of a great nation of Lycians.
Menestheus, Peteos' son, saw them and shuddered,   *345*
For they were advancing toward his part of the wall
And bringing ruin with them. Menestheus
Looked along the wall for a Greek captain
Who would be able to avert this disaster.
He saw both Ajaxes, who never seemed to tire,      *350*
And Teucer, who had just come from his hut.
They were near enough, but there was no way
To make a shout reach them, not with all the noise
Filling the air, the crash of shields and helmets
And the pounding on the gates, which were all closed now  *355*

And before each one of which the enemy stood,
Trying their best to break them and enter.
So Menestheus turned to the herald Thoötes:

"Run, Thoötes, and call Ajax, or better yet
Call both of them. All hell is going to break loose here.                360
The Lycian leaders are bearing down on us,
And they've been awfully tough in the big battles.
If the fighting is too heavy for them both to come,
At least get Telamonian Ajax here,
And Teucer too, who is good with a bow."                                  365

And the herald was off, running along the wall
Until he came to the two Ajaxes, to whom he said:

"My lords Ajax, captains of the Achaeans,
The son of Peteos, nurtured of Zeus,
Bids you come make a stand, however briefly,                             370
In the battle there–both of you would be best—
Since all hell is going to break loose there.
The Lycian leaders are bearing down on us,
And they've been awfully tough in the big battles.
If the fighting is too heavy for both of you to leave,                   375
At least let Telamonian Ajax come,
And Teucer too, who is good with a bow."

Telamonian Ajax heard the herald out
And said to his Oïlean counterpart:

"Ajax, stay here with Lycomedes                                          380
And keep these Danaans in the fight.
I'm going to make a stand over there.
When I've helped them out I'll come back here."

Big Ajax left, and with him Teucer,
His natural brother, and Pandion,                                        385
Who carried Teucer's curved bow.
Moving along the inside of the wall
They came to Menestheus' sector—

And to men hard-pressed. The Lycians
Were swarming up the battlements                                    *390*
Like black wind. The Greeks pushed back
With a shout. In the combat that ensued
It was Telamonian Ajax who first killed his man,
Sarpedon's comrade Epicles, hitting him
With a jagged piece of marble that lay on top                       *395*
Of the heap of stones inside the wall there.
You couldn't find a man alive now
Who could lift that stone with both hands,
But Ajax swung it high and hurled it
With enough force to shatter the four-horned helmet                 *400*
And crush Epicles' skull inside. He fell
As if he were doing a high dive from the wall,
And his spirit left his bones. Then Teucer hit
A fast charging Glaucus with an arrow
Where he saw his arm exposed. This stopped him cold,               *405*
And he leapt back from the wall, hiding his wound
From Greek eyes and his pride from their taunts.
It pained Sarpedon to see Glaucus withdraw
But it didn't take away any of his fight.
He hit Alcmaon, son of Thestor, with his spear,                    *410*
Jabbing it in, and as he pulled it out again
Alcmaon came forward with it, falling headfirst
And landing with a clatter of finely tooled bronze.
Sarpedon wrapped his hands around the battlement
And pulled. The whole section gave way, exposing                   *415*
The wall above and making an entrance for many.

Ajax and Teucer attacked him together.
Teucer's arrow hit his shield's bright belt
Where it slung across his chest, but Zeus
Beat off the death spirits. He would not allow                     *420*
His son to fall by the ships. Big Ajax
Leapt upon him at the same moment,
Thrusting his spear into Sarpedon's shield,
But could not push the point through.
He did make him reel backward, though.                             *425*

Sarpedon collected himself a short distance
Back from the wall. He was not giving up.
His heart still hoped to win glory here.
Wheeling around he called to his godlike Lycians:

"Lycians! Why are you slacking off from the fight?      430
Do you think I can knock this wall down alone
And clear a path to the ships? Help me out here.
The more men we have the better the work will go."

The Lycians cowered before their warlord's rebuke,
Then tightened the ranks around him even more.      435
The Greeks strengthened their positions on the wall
And steeled themselves for a major battle.
For all their strength the Lycians were unable
To break the wall, nor could the Greek spearmen
Push them back once they were close in.      440
They fought at close quarters,

                    *like two men*
    *Disputing boundary stones in a common field*
    *And defending their turf with the measuring rods*
    *They had brought with them to stake their claims.*      445

Likewise the Trojans and Greeks, separated
By the palisade and reaching over it
To hack away at each other's leather shields.
Many were wounded, mostly those who turned
Their unprotected backs to the enemy,      450
But many through their shields too, until
The whole wooden wall dripped with the blood
Of soldiers from both sides. But the Trojans
Could do nothing to drive the Greeks back.

    *An honest woman who works with her hands*      455
    *To bring home a meager wage for her children*
    *Will balance a weight of wool in her scales*
    *Until both pans are perfectly level.*

    So too this battle,
Until Zeus exalted Priam's son Hector,                          *460*
First to penetrate the Achaean wall.

His shout split the air:

                    "Move, Trojans!
Let's tear down this Greek fence
And make a bonfire out of their ships!"                         *465*

They heard him, all right, and swarmed
Right up the wall, climbing to its pickets
With spears in their hands, while Hector
Scooped up a stone that lay by the gates,
A massive boulder tapering to a point.                          *470*
It would take two men to heave it onto a cart—
More than two as men are now—but Hector
Handled it easily alone. Zeus
Lightened it for him, so that the stone
Was no more to Hector than the fleece                           *475*
Of a ram is to a shepherd who carries it
Easily in his free hand. This was how
Hector carried it up to the gates,
A set of heavy double doors, solidly built
And bolted shut by interlocked inner bars.                      *480*
Standing close to these towering doors, Hector
Spread his feet to get his weight behind the throw
And smashed the stone right into the middle.
The hinges broke off, and the stone's momentum
Carried it through, exploding the doors                         *485*
And sending splintered wood in every direction.
Hector jumped through, a spear in each hand.

His face was like sudden night,
And a dark gold light played about the armor
That encased his zealous bones. No one                          *490*
Could have stopped him, except the gods,
In his immortal leap through the ruined gate,
And his eyes glowed with fire.

Wheeling around
In the throng, Hector called to his Trojans,                    *495*
Who needed no persuasion, to scale the wall.
Those who couldn't, swarmed through the gate.
And the Greeks? In rout to their hollow ships,
With a noise like the damned stampeded into hell.

*[Books 13 through 15 are omitted. Poseidon rallies the Greeks. The Greek heroes Idomeneus and Meriones meet behind the lines, and then Idomeneus distinguishes himself in battle. The fighting is furious on both sides. The Greeks rout the Trojans, and Ajax knocks out Hector with a huge stone. Hera seduces Zeus to divert his attention from the Greeks' success. When Zeus awakes he aids Hector and the Trojans, and they advance all the way up to the Greek ships. Ajax alone holds the Trojans at bay as they attempt to burn one of the ships.]*

# ILIAD 16

While they fought for this ship, Patroclus
Came to Achilles and stood by him weeping,
His face like a sheer rock where the goat trails end
And dark springwater washes down the stone.
Achilles pitied him and spoke these feathered words:          *5*

"What are all these tears about, Patroclus?
You're like a little girl, pestering her mother
To pick her up, pulling at her hem
As she tries to hurry off and looking up at her
With tears in her eyes until she gets her way.          *10*
That's just what you look like, you know.
You have something to tell the Myrmidons?
Or myself? Bad news from back home?
Last I heard, Menoetius, your father,

And Peleus, mine, were still alive and well.                           *15*
Their deaths would indeed give us cause to grieve.
Or are you broken-hearted because some Greeks
Are being beaten dead beside our ships?
They had it coming. Out with it, Patroclus—
Don't try to hide it. I have a right to know."                         *20*

And with a deep groan you said to him,
Patroclus:

   "Achilles, great as you are,
Don't be vengeful. They are dying out there,
All of our best—or who used to be our best—                           *25*
They've all been hit and are lying
Wounded in camp. Diomedes is out,
And Odysseus, a good man with a spear,
Even Agamemnon has taken a hit.
Eurypylus, too, an arrow in his thigh.                                 *30*
The medics are working on them right now,
Stitching up their wounds. But you are incurable,
Achilles. God forbid I ever feel the spite
You nurse in your heart. You and your damned
Honor! What good will it do future generations                        *35*
If you let us go down to this defeat
In cold blood? Peleus was never your father
Or Thetis your mother. No, the grey sea spat you out
Onto crags in the surf, with an icy scab for a soul.
 What is it? If some secret your mother                           *40*
Has learned from Zeus is holding you back,
At least send *me* out, let *me* lead a troop
Of Myrmidons and light the way for our army.
And let me wear your armor. If the Trojans think
I am you, they'll back off and give the Greeks                        *45*
Some breathing space, what little there is in war.
Our rested men will turn them with a shout
And push them back from our ships to Troy."

 That was how Patroclus, like a child
Begging for a toy, begged for death.                                  *50*

And Achilles, angry and deeply troubled:

"Ah, my noble friend, what a thing to say.
No, I'm not in on any divine secret,
Nor has my mother told me anything from Zeus.
But I take it hard when someone in power                    55
Uses his authority to rob his equal
And strip him of his honor. I take it hard.
The girl the Greeks chose to be my prize—
After I demolished a walled city to get her—
Lord Agamemnon, son of Atreus, just took                    60
From my hands, as if I were some tramp.
    But we'll let that be. I never meant
To hold my grudge forever. But I did say
I would not relent from my anger until
The noise of battle lapped at my own ships' hulls.          65
So it's on your shoulders now. Wear my armor
And lead our Myrmidons into battle,
If it is true that a dark cloud of Trojans
Has settled in over the ships and the Greeks
Are hemmed in on a narrow strip of beach.                   70
The Trojans have become cocky, the whole city,
Because they do not see my helmeted face
Flaring close by. They would retreat so fast
They would clog the ditches with their dead—
If Lord Agamemnon knew how to respect me.                   75
As it is they have brought the war to our camp.
So Diomedes is out, eh? It was his inspired
Spear work that kept the Trojans at arm's length.
And I haven't been hearing Agamemnon's battle cry,
As much as I hate the throat it comes from—only            80
Hector's murderous shout breaking like the sea
Over the Trojans, urging them on. The whole plain
Is filled with their whooping as they rout the Greeks.
    Hit them hard, Patroclus, before they burn the ships
And leave us stranded here. But before you go,              85
Listen carefully to every word I say.
Win me my honor, my glory and my honor
From all the Greeks, and, as their restitution,

The girl Briseis, and many other gifts.
But once you've driven the Trojans from the ships,                    *90*
You come back, no matter how much
Hera's thundering husband lets you win.
Any success you have against the Trojans
Will be at the expense of my honor.
And if you get so carried away                                        *95*
With killing the Trojans that you press on to Troy,
One of the immortals may intervene.
Apollo, for one, loves them dearly.
So once you have made some daylight for the ships,
You come back where you belong.                                       *100*
The others can fight it out on the plain.
    O Patroclus, I wish to Father Zeus
    And to Athena and Apollo
That all of them, Greeks and Trojans alike,
Every last man on Troy's dusty plain,                                 *105*
Were dead, and only you and I were left
    To rip Ilion down, stone by sacred stone."

And while they talked, Ajax retreated.

Zeus saw to it that everything the Trojans threw
At Ajax hit him, and his helmet tickered and rang                     *110*
From all the metal points its bronze deflected
From his temples and cheeks. His left arm was sore
From holding up his shield, but the Trojans could not,
For all their pressure, force it aside.
Gulping in air, sweat pouring down his limbs,                         *115*
He could scarcely breathe and had nowhere to turn.

Tell me now, Muses, who dwell on Olympus,
How fire first fell on the Achaean ships.

It was Hector who forced his way
To Ajax's side, and with his heavy sword                              *120*
Lopped through the ash-wood shaft of his spear
At the socket's base, sending the bronze point
Clanging onto the ground far behind him

And leaving in Ajax's hands a blunted stick.
Ajax knew that this was the work of the gods,                     *125*
That Zeus had cancelled Ajax's battle plans
And planned instead a Trojan victory.
No one could blame him for getting out of range,
And when he did, the Trojans threw their firebrands
Onto the ship, and she went up in flames.                        *130*

Achilles slapped his thighs and said:

"Hurry, Patroclus! I see fire from the ships.
Don't let them take the fleet and cut off our escape.
Put on the armor while I gather the troops."

And so Patroclus armed, putting on                                *135*
The bronze metalwork tailored to the body
Of Aeacus' swift grandson: the greaves
Trimmed with silver at the ankles, the corselet
Spangled with stars, the silver-studded sword,
The massive shield, and the crested helmet                       *140*
That made every nod a threat.
He took two spears of the proper heft,
But left behind the massive battle pike
Of Aeacus' incomparable grandson.
No one but Achilles could handle this spear,                     *145*
Made of ash, which the centaur Chiron
Had brought down from Mount Pelion and given
To Achilles' father to be the death of heroes.
Patroclus left the horses to Automedon,
The warrior he trusted most, after Achilles,                     *150*
To be at his side in the crush of battle.
Automedon led beneath the yoke
The windswift horses Xanthus and Balius,
Immortal horses the gods gave to Peleus
When he married silver Thetis.                                    *155*
The Harpy Podarge had conceived them
When the West Wind blew through her
As she grazed in a meadow near Ocean's stream.
As trace horse Automedon brought up Pedasus,

Whom Achilles had acquired in the raid                    *160*
On Eëtion's city. This faultless animal,
Though mortal, kept pace with immortal horses.

Achilles toured the rows of huts
That composed the Myrmidons' camp
And saw to it the men got armed.                          *165*

    *Think of wolves*
*Ravenous for meat. It is impossible*
*To describe their savage strength in the hunt,*
*But after they have killed an antlered stag*
*Up in the hills and torn it apart, they come down*       *170*
*With gore on their jowls, and in a pack*
*Go to lap the black surface water in a pool*
*Fed by a dark spring, and as they drink,*
*Crimson curls float off from their slender tongues.*
*But their hearts are still, and their bellies gorged.*   *175*

So too the Myrmidon commanders
Flanking Achilles' splendid surrogate,
And in their midst stood Achilles himself,
Urging on the horses and the men.

Achilles had brought fifty ships to Troy.                 *180*
Each ship held fifty men, and the entire force
Was divided into five battalions
Whose five commanders answered to Achilles.
    Menesthius led the first battalion.
His mother, Polydore, a daughter of Peleus,               *185*
Had lain with the river god Spercheius,
Whose sky-swollen waters engendered the child.
His nominal father was a man called Boros,
Who gave many gifts to marry Polydore.
    The second battalion was led by Eudorus,   *190*
Polymele's bastard son. This woman
Once caught Hermes' eye as she danced
In Artemis' choir, and the god later
Went up to her bedroom and slept with her.

The son she bore shone like silver in battle.                    *195*
After childbirth Actor's son Echecles
Led her to his house in marriage,
And her father, Phylas, kept the boy
And brought him up as if he were his own.
  Peisander led the third contingent.                  *200*
He was, next to Patroclus, the best
Of all the Myrmidons with a spear.
  Old Phoenix led the fourth contingent,
And Alcimedon, Laerces' son, the fifth.

  When Achilles had the troops assembled               *205*
By battalions, he spoke to them bluntly:

"Myrmidons! I would not have a man among you forget
The threats you have been issuing against the Trojans—
From the safety of our camp—while I was in my rage.
All this time you have been calling me                           *210*
The hard-boiled son of Peleus and saying to my face
That my mother must have weaned me on gall
Or I wouldn't keep my friends from battle.
That, together with hints you'd sail back home
If all I was going to do was sit and sulk. Now, however,         *215*
That there *is* a major battle to hold your interest,
I hope that each of you remembers what it means to fight."

The speech steeled their spirit. The Myrmidons
Closed ranks until there was no more space between them
Than between the stones a mason sets in the wall                 *220*
Of a high house when he wants to seal it from the wind.
Helmet on helmet, shield overlapping shield, man on man,
So close the horsehair plumes on their bright crests
Rubbed each other as their heads bobbed up and down.
And in front of them all, two men with one heart,               *225*
Patroclus and Automedon made their final preparations
To lead the Myrmidons into war.
       But Achilles
Went back to his hut and opened the lid
Of a beautiful, carved chest his mother Thetis                   *230*

Had put aboard his ship when he sailed for Troy,
Filled with tunics and cloaks and woolen rugs.
And in it too was a chalice that no one else
Ever drank from, and that he alone used for libation
To no other god but Zeus. This chalice                                    *235*
He now took from the chest, purified it
With sulfur crystals, washed it with clear water,
Then cleansed his hands and filled it with bright red wine.
And then he prayed, standing in his courtyard
Pouring out the wine as he looked up to heaven.                           *240*
And as he prayed, Zeus in his thunderhead listened.

"Lord Zeus, God of Dodona, Pelasgian God
Who dwells afar in the snows of Dodona
With your barefoot priests who sleep
On the ground around your sacred oak:                                     *245*
As you have heard my prayer before
And did honor me and smite the Achaeans,
So now too fulfill my prayer.
As I wait in the muster of the ships
And send my Patroclus into battle with my men,                           *250*
Send forth glory with him.
Make bold the heart in his breast
So that Hector will see that my comrade
Knows how to fight and win without me.
And when he has driven the noise of battle                               *255*
Away from our ships, may he come back to me
Unharmed, with all his weapons and men."

Zeus in his wisdom heard Achilles' prayer
And granted half of it. Yes, Patroclus
Would drive the Trojans back from the ships,                             *260*
But he would not return from battle unharmed.

Achilles placed the chalice back in the chest
And stood outside his hut. He still longed to see
The grim struggle on Troy's windswept plain.

 The Myrmidons under Patroclus                                           *265*

Filed out and swarmed up to the Trojans.

> *Boys will sometimes disturb a hornets' nest*
> *By the roadside, jabbing at it and infuriating*
> *The hive—the little fools—*
> *Until the insects become a menace to all*                    270
> *And attack any traveller who happens by,*
> *Swarming out in defense of their brood.*

So too the Myrmidons.
Patroclus called to them over their shouts:

"Remember whose men you are                                     275
And for whose honor you are fighting.
And fight so that even wide-ruling Agamemnon
Will recognize his blind folly
In not honoring the best of the Achaeans.
    FOR ACHILLES!"                                              280

This raised their spirits even higher.
They were all over the Trojans,
And the ships' hulls reverberated
With the sounds of their battle cries.
The Trojans, when they saw Patroclus                            285
Gleaming in his armor, fell apart,
Convinced that Achilles had come out at last,
His wrath renounced and solidarity restored.
Each of them looked for a way to save his skin.

Patroclus' spear shot out like stabbing light                  290
To where the Trojans were clustered
Around the stern of Protesilaus' ship
And hit a certain chariot commander
Named Pyraechmes, a Paeonian
Who had led a contingent of chariots                            295
From the Axius river in Amydon.
He went down now, groaning in the dust
With Patroclus' spear in his right shoulder.
Having lost their leader and best fighter

The Paeonians panicked, and Patroclus                          300
Drove them from the ships and doused the fire.

The half-burnt ship was left there.

                                 The Trojans,
Frantic and screaming, were on the run,
And the Greeks poured in with an answering roar.               305

   *Zeus will at times rein in his lightning*
   *And remove a dense cloud from a mountain top,*
   *And all the crests and headlands and high glades*
   *Break into view, and brightness falls from the air.*

The Greeks had repelled the enemy fire                         310
From the ships and could catch their breath,
But only for a while. The battle was not over.
The Trojans had withdrawn from the black ships,
But were not giving up. They had taken a stand
And would have to be pushed back by force.                     315
The fighting was scattered at first, as heroes
Killed each other in individual combat.

[Lines 318–80 are omitted. The fighting continues.]

All this time big Ajax was trying
To get a shot off at Hector, who,
Knowing the ways of war, kept his shoulders
Under his oxhide shield and listened
For the whistling of arrows and thud of spears.                385
He knew the fight was not going his way,
But he held his ground and tried to save his friends.

   *A cloud detaches itself from Olympus*
   *And moves across the clear blue sky*
   *When Zeus is about to unleash a storm.*                 390

The rout from the ships had begun,

And in no good order. Hector's horses
Got him across the trench, but he left
His army behind it. The Trojans drove
Team after team into the trench                                    395
Only to see the horses break their poles,
Struggle free, and leave their lords
Stranded in their chariots. Patroclus
Called his men in for the kill. The Trojans
Were screaming and running                                         400
In every direction, while a cloud of dust
Rose high over their horses as they left
The ships behind and strained for the city.
Patroclus drove his chariot to wherever
The routed Trojans were thickest,                                  405
Shouting as he plowed over broken chariots
And the drivers who fell beneath his wheels.
The horses the gods had given to Peleus
Jumped the trench in one immortal leap,
And Patroclus steered them after Hector,                           410
In whose back he longed to plant his spear,
But Hector's horses had too big a lead.

> *When the storm finally breaks, on a day*
> *During harvest, the black earth is soaked*
> *Until it can hold no more, and still the rain*          415
> *Comes down in sheets as Zeus' judgment*
> *On men who govern by violence*
> *And drive Justice out with their crooked verdicts,*
> *As if they have never heard of an Angry God.*
> *All the rivers flood their banks, and every hill*       420
> *Is rutted with torrents that feed the rivers,*
> *And down from the mountains the waters roar*
> *And sweep men's tillage into the shining sea.*

The Trojan mares were thundering down the plain.

Patroclus let them go. But when he had cut off             425
The foremost battalions, he hemmed them back
Toward the ships, blocking their frantic retreat

Toward the city, and in the space defined
By the ships, the river, and Troy's high wall,
   He made them pay in blood.                                                      *430*


[Lines 431–54 are omitted. Patroclus routs the Lycians.]

Sarpedon saw his comrades running                                             *455*
With their tunics flapping loose around their waists
And being swatted down like flies by Patroclus.
He called out, appealing to their sense of shame:


"Why this sudden burst of speed, Lycian heroes?
Slow down a little, while I make the acquaintance                         *460*
Of this nuisance of a Greek who seems by now
To have hamstrung half the Trojan army."


And he stepped down from his chariot in his bronze
As Patroclus, seeing him, stepped down from his.


   *High above a cliff vultures are screaming*                               *465*
   *In the air as they savage each other's craws*
   *With their hooked beaks and talons.*


   And higher still,
Zeus watched with pity as the two heroes closed
And said to his wife Hera, who is his sister too:                           *470*


"Fate has it that Sarpedon, whom I love more
Than any man, is to be killed by Patroclus.
Shall I take him out of battle while he still lives
And set him down in the rich land of Lycia,
Or shall I let him die under Patroclus' hands?"                         *475*


And Hera, his lady, her eyes soft and wide:


"Son of Cronus, what a thing to say!
A mortal man, whose fate has long been fixed,
And you want to save him from rattling death?

Do it. But don't expect all of us to approve.                    480
Listen to me. If you send Sarpedon home alive,
You will have to expect other gods to do the same
And save their own sons—and there are many of them
In this war around Priam's great city.
Think of the resentment you will create.                         485
But if you love him and are filled with grief,
Let him fall in battle at Patroclus' hands,
And when his soul and life have left him,
Send Sleep and Death to bear him away
To Lycia, where his people will give him burial                  490
With mound and stone, as befits the dead."

The Father of Gods and Men agreed
Reluctantly, but shed drops of blood as rain
Upon the earth in honor of his own dear son
Whom Patroclus was about to kill                                 495
On Ilion's rich soil, far from his native land.
When they were close, Patroclus cast, and hit
Not Prince Sarpedon, but his lieutenant
Thrasymelus, a good man—a hard throw
Into the pit of his belly. He collapsed in a heap.              500
Sarpedon countered and missed. His bright spear
Sliced instead through the right shoulder
Of Pedasus, who gave one pained, rasping whinny,
Then fell in the dust. His spirit fluttered off.
With the trace horse down, the remaining two                     505
Struggled in the creaking yoke, tangling the reins.
Automedon remedied this by drawing his sword
And cutting loose the trace horse. The other two
Righted themselves and pulled hard at the reins,
And the two warriors closed again in mortal combat.             510
Sarpedon cast again. Another miss. The spearpoint
Glinted as it sailed over Patroclus' left shoulder
Without touching him at all. Patroclus came back,
Leaning into his throw, and the bronze point
Caught Sarpedon just below the rib cage                          515
Where it protects the beating heart. Sarpedon fell

*As a tree falls, oak, or poplar, or spreading pine,*
*When carpenters cut it down in the forest*
*With their bright axes, to be the beam of a ship,*

And he lay before his horses and chariot,                          *520*
Groaning heavily and clawing the bloody dust,

*Like some tawny, spirited bull a lion has killed*
*In the middle of the shambling herd, groaning*
*As it dies beneath the predator's jaws.*

Thus beneath Patroclus the Lycian commander                        *525*
Struggled in death. And he called his friend:

"Glaucus, it's time to show what you're made of
And be the warrior you've always been,
Heart set on evil war—if you're fast enough.
Hurry, rally our best to fight for my body,                         *530*
All the Lycian leaders. Shame on you,
Glaucus, until your dying day, if the Greeks
Strip my body bare beside their ships.
Be strong and keep the others going."

The end came as he spoke, and death settled                         *535*
On his nostrils and eyes. Patroclus put his heel
On Sarpedon's chest and pulled out his spear.
The lungs came out with it, and Sarpedon's life.
The Myrmidons steadied his snorting horses.
They did not want to leave their master's chariot.                  *540*

Glaucus could hardly bear to hear Sarpedon's voice,
He was so grieved that he could not save him.
He pressed his arm with his hand. His wound
Tormented him, the wound he got when Teucer
Shot him with an arrow as he attacked the wall.                     *545*
He prayed to Apollo, Lord of bright distances:

"Hear me, O Lord, wherever you are
In Lycia or Troy, for everywhere you hear

Men in their grief, and grief has come to me.
I am wounded, Lord, my arm is on fire,                    550
And the blood can't be staunched. My shoulder
Is so sore I cannot hold a steady spear
And fight the enemy. Sarpedon is dead,
My Lord, and Zeus will not save his own son.
Heal my wound and deaden my pain,                    555
And give me the strength to call the Lycians
And urge them on to fight, and do battle myself
About the body of my fallen comrade."

Thus Glaucus' prayer, and Apollo heard him.
He stilled his pain and staunched the dark blood                    560
That flowed from his wound. Glaucus felt
The god's strength pulsing through him,
Glad that his prayers were so quickly answered.
He rounded up the Lycian leaders
And urged them to fight for Sarpedon's body,                    565
Then went with long strides to the Trojans,
To Polydamas, Agenor, Aeneas,
And then saw Hector's bronze-strapped face,
Went up to him and said levelly:

"Hector, you have abandoned your allies.                    570
We have been putting our lives on the line for you
Far from our homes and loved ones,
And you don't care enough to lend us aid.
Sarpedon is down, our great warlord,
Whose word in Lycia was Lycia's law,                    575
Killed by Patroclus under Ares' prodding.
Show some pride and fight for his body,
Or the Myrmidons will strip off the armor
And defile his corpse, in recompense
For all the Greeks we have killed by the ships."                    580

This was almost too much for the Trojans.
Sarpedon, though a foreigner, had been
A mainstay of their city, the leader
Of a large force and its best fighter.

Hector led them straight at the Greeks,                          *585*
  "For Sarpedon!"

[Lines 587–666 are omitted. The fighting continues.]

The plain of Troy thrummed with the sound
Of bronze and hide stretched into shields,
And of swords and spears knifing into these.
Sarpedon's body was indistinguishable                           *670*
From the blood and grime and splintered spears
That littered his body from head to foot.

  *But if you have ever seen how flies*
  *Cluster about the brimming milk pails*
  *On a dairy farm in early summer,*                            *675*

You will have some idea of the throng
Around Sarpedon's corpse.

                          And not once did Zeus
Avert his luminous eyes from the combatants.
All this time he looked down at them and pondered               *680*
When Patroclus should die, whether
Shining Hector should kill him then and there
In the conflict over godlike Sarpedon
And strip the armor from his body, or whether
He should live to destroy even more Trojans.                    *685*
And as he pondered it seemed preferable
That Achilles' spendid surrogate should once more
Drive the Trojans and bronze-helmed Hector
Back to the city, and take many lives.
And Hector felt it, felt his blood turn milky,                  *690*
And mounted his chariot, calling to the others
To begin the retreat, that Zeus' scales were tipping.
Not even the Lycians stayed, not with Sarpedon
Lying at the bottom of a pile of bodies
That had fallen upon him in this node of war.                   *695*

The Greeks stripped at last the glowing bronze
From Sarpedon's shoulders, and Patroclus gave it
To some of his comrades to take back to the ships.

Then Zeus turned to Apollo and said:

"Sun God, take our Sarpedon out of range.                    700
Cleanse his wounds of all the clotted blood,
And wash him in the river far away
And anoint him with our holy chrism
And wrap the body in a deathless shroud
And give him over to be taken swiftly                        705
  By Sleep and Death to Lycia,
Where his people shall give him burial
With mound and stone, as befits the dead."

And Apollo went down from Ida
Into the howling dust of war,                                710
And cleansed Sarpedon's wounds of all the blood,
And washed him in the river far away
And anointed him with holy chrism
And wrapped the body in a deathless shroud
And gave him over to be taken swiftly                        715
  By Sleep and Death to Lycia.

Patroclus called to his horses and charioteer
And pressed on after the Trojans and Lycians,
Forgetting everything Achilles had said
And mindless of the black fates gathering above.            720
Even then you might have escaped them,
Patroclus, but Zeus' mind is stronger than men's,
And Zeus now put fury in your heart.

Do you remember it, Patroclus, all the Trojans
You killed as the gods called you to your death?            725
Adrastus was first, then Autonous, and Echeclus,
Perimas, son of Megas, Epistor, Melanippus,
Elasus, Mulius, and last, Pylartes,
And it would have been more, but the others ran,

Back to Troy, which would have fallen that day                    730
By Patroclus' hands.

                But Phoebus Apollo
Had taken his stand on top of Troy's wall.

Three times Patroclus
Reached the parapet, and three times                              735
Apollo's fingers flicked against the human's shield
And pushed him off. But when he came back
A fourth time, like a spirit from beyond,
Apollo's voice split the daylight in two:

"Get back, Patroclus, back where you belong.                      740
Troy is fated to fall, but not to you,
Nor even to Achilles, a better man by far."

And Patroclus was off, putting distance
Between himself and that wrathful voice.

  Hector had halted his horses at the Western Gate        745
And was deciding whether to drive back into battle
Or call for a retreat to within the walls.
While he pondered this, Phoebus Apollo
Came up to him in the guise of Asius.
This man was Hector's uncle on his mother's side,               750
And Apollo looked just like him as he spoke:

"Why are you out of action, Hector? It's not right.
If I were as much stronger than you as I am weaker,
You'd pay dearly for withdrawing from battle.
Get in that chariot and go after Patroclus.                      755
Who knows? Apollo may give you the glory."

Hector commanded Cebriones, his charioteer,
To whip the horses into battle. Apollo melted
Into the throng, a god into the toil of men.
The Greeks felt a sudden chill,                                   760
While Hector and the Trojans felt their spirits lift.

Hector was not interested in the other Greeks.
He drove through them and straight for Patroclus,
Who leapt down from his own chariot
With a spear in one hand and in the other                        765
A jagged piece of granite he had scooped up
And now cupped in his palm. He got set,
And without more than a moment of awe
For who his opponent was, hurled the stone.
The throw was not wasted. He hit Hector's                        770
Charioteer, Cebriones, Priam's bastard son,
As he stood there holding the reins. The sharp stone
Caught him right in the forehead, smashing
His brows together and shattering the skull
So that his eyeballs spurted out and dropped                     775
Into the dirt before his feet. He flipped backward
From the chariot like a diver, and his soul
Dribbled away from his bones. And you,
Patroclus, you, my horseman, mocked him:

"What a spring the man has! Nice dive!                           780
Think of the oysters he could come up with
If he were out at sea, jumping off the boat
In all sorts of weather, to judge by the dive
He just took from his chariot onto the plain."

And with that he rushed at the fallen warrior                   785

> *Like a lion who has been wounded in the chest*
> *As he ravages a farmstead, and his own valor*
> *Destroys him.*

                    Yes, Patroclus, that is how you leapt
Upon Cebriones.                                                 790
                  Hector vaulted from his chariot,
And the two of them fought over Cebriones

> *Like a pair of lions fighting over a slain deer*
> *In the high mountains, both of them ravenous,*
> *Both high of heart,*                                          795

                              very much like these two
Human heroes hacking at each other with bronze.
Hector held Cebriones' head and would not let go.
Patroclus had hold of a foot, and around them
Greeks and Trojans squared off and fought.                          *800*

> *Winds sometimes rise in a deep mountain wood*
> *From different directions, and the trees—*
> *Beech, ash, and cornelian cherry—*
> *Batter each other with their long, tapered branches,*
> *And you can hear the sound from a long way off,*          *805*
> *The unnerving splintering of hardwood limbs.*

The Trojans and Greeks collided in battle,
And neither side thought of yielding ground.

Around Cebriones many spears were stuck,
Many arrows flew singing from the string,                           *810*
And many stones thudded onto the shields
Of men fighting around him. But there he lay
In the whirling dust, one of the great,
    Forgetful of his horsemanship.

While the sun still straddled heaven's meridian,                    *815*
Soldiers on both sides were hit and fell.
But when the sun moved down the sky and men
All over earth were unyoking their oxen,
The Greeks' success exceeded their destiny.
They pulled Cebriones from the Trojan lines                         *820*
And out of range, and stripped his armor.

And then Patroclus unleashed himself.

Three times he charged into the Trojan ranks
With the raw power of Ares, yelling coldly,
And on each charge he killed nine men.                              *825*
But when you made your fourth, demonic charge,
Then—did you feel it, Patroclus?—out of the mist,
Your death coming to meet you. It was

Apollo, whom you did not see in the thick of battle,
Standing behind you, and the flat of his hand                  *830*
Found the space between your shoulder blades.
The sky's blue disk went spinning in your eyes
As Achilles' helmet rang beneath the horses' hooves,
And rolled in the dust—no, that couldn't be right—
Those handsome horsehair plumes grimed with blood,             *835*
The gods would never let that happen to the helmet
That had protected the head and graceful brow
Of divine Achilles. But the gods did
Let it happen, and Zeus would now give the helmet
To Hector, whose own death was not far off.                    *840*

Nothing was left of Patroclus' heavy battle spear
But splintered wood, his tasselled shield and baldric
Fell to the ground, and Apollo, Prince of the Sky,
Split loose his breastplate. And he stood there, naked,
Astounded, his silvery limbs floating away,                    *845*
Until one of the Trojans slipped up behind him
And put his spear through, a boy named Euphorbus,
The best his age with a spear, mounted or on foot.
He had already distinguished himself in this war
By knocking twenty warriors out of their cars                  *850*
The first time he went out for chariot lessons.
It was this boy who took his chance at you,
Patroclus, but instead of finishing you off,
He pulled his spear out and ran back where he belonged,
Unwilling to face even an unarmed Patroclus,                   *855*
Who staggered back toward his comrades, still alive,
But overcome by the god's stroke, and the spear.

Hector was watching this, and when he saw
Patroclus withdrawing with a wound, he muscled
His way through to him and rammed his spearhead               *860*
Into the pit of his belly and all the way through.
Patroclus fell heavily. You could hear the Greeks wince.

   *A boar does not wear out easily, but a lion*
   *Will overpower it when the two face off*

*Over a trickling spring up in the mountains*                    865
*They both want to drink from. The boar*
*Pants hard, but the lion comes out on top.*

So too did Hector, whose spear was draining the life
From Menoetius' son, who had himself killed many.

His words beat down on Patroclus like dark wings:                870

"So, Patroclus, you thought you could ransack my city
And ship our women back to Greece to be your slaves.
You little fool. They are defended by me,
By Hector, by my horses and my spear. I am the one,
Troy's best, who keeps their doom at bay. But you,             875
Patroclus, the vultures will eat you
On this very spot. Your marvelous Achilles
Has done you no good at all. I can just see it,
Him sitting in his tent and telling you as you left:
'Don't bother coming back to the ships,                         880
Patroclus, until you have ripped Hector's heart out
Through his bloody shirt.' That's what he said,
Isn't it? And you were stupid enough to listen."

And Patroclus, barely able to shake the words out:

"Brag while you can, Hector. Zeus and Apollo                    885
Have given you an easy victory this time.
If they hadn't knocked off my armor,
I could have made mincemeat of twenty like you.
It was Fate, and Leto's son, who killed me.
Of men, Euphorbus. You came in third at best.                  890
And one more thing for you to think over.
You're not going to live long. I see Death
Standing at your shoulder, and you going down
Under the hands of Peleus' perfect son."

Death's veil covered him as he said these things,              895
And his soul, bound for Hades, fluttered out
Resentfully, forsaking manhood's bloom.

He was dead when Hector said to him:

"Why prophesy my death, Patroclus?
Who knows? Achilles, son of Thetis,                    *900*
May go down first under my spear."

And propping his heel against the body,
He extracted his bronze spear and took off
After Automedon. But Automedon was gone,
Pulled by immortal horses, the splendid gifts         *905*
The gods once gave to Peleus.

*[Book 17 is omitted. There is a desperate struggle over the corpse of Patroclus. The Greeks send Antilochus to bring the news to Achilles.]*

# ILIAD 18

The fight went on, like wildfire burning.
Antilochus, running hard like a herald,
Found Achilles close to his upswept hulls,
His great heart brooding with premonitions
Of what had indeed already happened.                  *5*

"This looks bad,
All these Greeks with their hair in the wind
Stampeding off the plain and back to the ships.
God forbid that what my mother told me
Has now come true, that while I'm still alive         *10*
Trojan hands would steal the sunlight
From the best of all the Myrmidons.
Patroclus, Menoetius' brave son, is dead.
Damn him! I told him only to repel
The enemy fire from our ships,                        *15*

And not to take on Hector in a fight."

Antilochus was in tears when he reached him
And delivered his unendurable message:

"Son of wise Peleus, this is painful news
For you to hear, and I wish it were not true.                    20
Patroclus is down, and they are fighting
For his naked corpse. Hector has the armor."

A mist of black grief enveloped Achilles.
He scooped up fistfuls of sunburnt dust
And poured it on his head, fouling                              25
His beautiful face. Black ash grimed
His finespun cloak as he stretched his huge body
Out in the dust and lay there,
Tearing out his hair with his hands.
The women, whom Achilles and Patroclus                         30
Had taken in raids, ran shrieking out of the tent
To be with Achilles, and they beat their breasts
Until their knees gave out beneath them.
Antilochus, sobbing himself, stayed with Achilles
And held his hands—he was groaning                             35
From the depths of his soul—for fear
He would lay open his own throat with steel.

The sound of Achilles' grief stung the air.

Down in the water his mother heard him,
Sitting in the sea-depths beside her old father,               40
And she began to wail.
                 And the saltwater women
Gathered around her, all the deep-sea Nereids,
Glaucê and Thaleia and Cymodocê,
Neseia and Speio, Thoê and ox-eyed Haliê,                      45
Cymothoê, Actaeê, and Limnoeira,
Melitê and Iaera, Amphithoê and Agauê,
Doris, Panopê, and milk-white Galateia,
Nemertes, Apseudes, and Callianassa,

Clymenê, Ianeira, Ianassa, and Maera,                        *50*
Oreithyia and Amatheia, hair streaming behind her,
And all of the other deep-sea Nereids.
They filled the silver, shimmering cave,
And they all beat their breasts.

                              Thetis led the lament:          *55*

"Hear me, sisters, hear the pain in my heart.
I gave birth to a son, and that is my sorrow,
My perfect son, the best of heroes.
He grew like a sapling, and I nursed him
As I would a plant on the hill in my garden,       *60*
And I sent him to Ilion on a sailing ship
To fight the Trojans. And now I will never
Welcome him home again to Peleus' house.
As long as he lives and sees the sunlight
He will be in pain, and I cannot help him.         *65*
But I'll go now to see and hear my dear son,
Since he is suffering while he waits out the war."

She left the cave, and they went with her,
Weeping, and around them a wave
Broke through the sea, and they came to Troy.      *70*
They emerged on the beach where the Myrmidons' ships
Formed an encampment around Achilles.
He was groaning deeply, and his mother
Stood next to him and held her son's head.
Her lamentation hung sharp in the air,             *75*
And then she spoke in low, sorrowful tones:

"Child, why are you crying? What pain
Has come to your heart? Speak, don't hide it.
Zeus has granted your prayer. The Greeks
Have all been beaten back to their ships           *80*
And suffered horribly. They can't do without you."

Achilles answered her:

"Mother, Zeus may have done all this for me,
But how can I rejoice? My friend is dead,
Patroclus, my dearest friend of all. I loved him,                    85
And I killed him. And the armor—
Hector cut him down and took off his body
The heavy, splendid armor, beautiful to see,
That the gods gave to Peleus as a gift
On the day they put you to bed with a mortal.                        90
You should have stayed with the saltwater women,
And Peleus should have married a mortal.
But now—it was all so you would suffer pain
For your ravaged son. You will never again
Welcome me home, since I no longer have the will                     95
To remain alive among men, not unless Hector
Loses his life on the point of my spear
And pays for despoiling Menoetius' son."

And Thetis, in tears, said to him:

"I won't have you with me for long, my child,                        100
If you say such things. Hector's death means yours."

From under a great weight, Achilles answered:

"Then let me die now. I was no help
To him when he was killed out there. He died
Far from home, and he needed me to protect him.                     105
But now, since I'm not going home, and wasn't
A light for Patroclus or any of the rest
Of my friends who have been beaten by Hector,
But just squatted by my ships, a dead weight on the earth . . .
I stand alone in the whole Greek army                               110
When it comes to war—though some do speak better.
I wish all strife could stop, among gods
And among men, and anger too—it sends
Sensible men into fits of temper,
It drips down our throats sweeter than honey                        115
And mushrooms up in our bellies like smoke.
Yes, the warlord Agamemnon angered me.

But we'll let that be, no matter how it hurts,
And conquer our pride, because we must.
But I'm going now to find the man who destroyed                    120
My beloved—Hector.
                              As for my own fate,
I'll accept it whenever it pleases Zeus
And the other immortal gods to send it.
Not even Heracles could escape his doom.                           125
He was dearest of all to Lord Zeus, but fate
And Hera's hard anger destroyed him.
If it is true that I have a fate like his, then I too
Will lie down in death.
                              But now to win glory                 130
And make some Trojan woman or deep-breasted
Dardanian matron wipe the tears
From her soft cheeks, make her sob and groan.
Let them feel how long I've been out of the war.
Don't try, out of love, to stop me. I won't listen."              135

And Thetis, her feet silver on the sand:

"Yes, child. It's not wrong to save your friends
When they are beaten to the brink of death.
But your beautiful armor is in the hands of the Trojans,
The mirrored bronze. Hector himself                                140
Has it on his shoulders. He glories in it.
Not for long, though. I see his death is near.
But you, don't dive into the red dust of war
Until with your own eyes you see me returning.
Tomorrow I will come with the rising sun                           145
Bearing beautiful armor from Lord Hephaestus."

Thetis spoke, turned away
From her son, and said to her saltwater sisters:

"Sink now into the sea's wide lap
And go down to our old father's house                              150
And tell him all this. I am on my way
Up to Olympus to visit Hephaestus,

The glorious smith, to see if for my sake
He will give my son glorious armor."

As she spoke they dove into the waves,                               *155*
And the silver-footed goddess was gone
Off to Olympus to fetch arms for her child.

  And while her feet carried her off to Olympus,
Hector yelled, a yell so bloodcurdling and loud
It stampeded the Greeks all the way back                             *160*
To their ships beached on the Hellespont's shore.
They could not pull the body of Patroclus
Out of javelin range, and soon Hector,
With his horses and men, stood over it again.
Three times Priam's resplendent son                                  *165*
Took hold of the corpse's heels and tried
To drag it off, bawling commands to his men.
Three times the two Ajaxes put their heads down,
Charged, and beat him back. Unshaken, Hector
Sidestepped, cut ahead, or held his ground                          *170*
With a shout, but never yielded an inch.

    *It was like shepherds against a starving lion,*
      *Helpless to beat it back from a carcass,*

The two Ajaxes unable to rout
The son of Priam from Patroclus' corpse.                             *175*
And Hector would have, to his eternal glory,
Dragged the body off, had not Iris stormed
Down from Olympus with a message for Achilles,
Unbeknownst to Zeus and the other gods.
Hera had sent her, and this was her message:                        *180*

"Rise, son of Peleus, most formidable of men.
Rescue Patroclus, for whom a terrible battle
Is pitched by the ships, men killing each other,
Some fighting to save the dead man's body,
The Trojans trying to drag it back                                   *185*
To windy Ilion. Hector's mind especially

Is bent on this. He means to impale the head
On Troy's palisade after he strips off its skin.
And you just lie there? Think of Patroclus
Becoming a ragbone for Trojan dogs. Shame          *190*
To your dying day if his corpse is defiled."

The shining sprinter Achilles answered her:

"Iris, which god sent you here?"

And Iris, whose feet are wind, responded:

"None other than Hera, Zeus' glorious wife.         *195*
But Zeus on high does not know this, nor do
Any of the immortals on snow-capped Olympus."

And Achilles, the great runner:

"How can I go to war? They have my armor.
And my mother told me not to arm myself            *200*
Until with my own eyes I see her come back
With fine weapons from Hephaestus.
I don't know any other armor that would fit,
Unless maybe the shield of Telamonian Ajax.
But he's out there in the front ranks, I hope,      *205*
Fighting with his spear over Patroclus dead."

Windfoot Iris responded:

"We know very well that they have your armor.
Just go to the trench and let the Trojans see you.
One look will be enough. The Trojans will back off  *210*
Out of fear of you, and this will give the Greeks
Some breathing space, what little there is in war."

Iris spoke and was gone. And Achilles,
Whom the gods loved, rose. Around
His mighty shoulders Athena threw                   *215*
Her tasselled aegis, and the shining goddess

Haloed his head with a golden cloud
That shot flames from its incandescent glow.

> *Smoke is rising through the pure upper air*
> *From a besieged city on a distant island.*                    220
> *Its soldiers have fought hard all day,*
> *But at sunset they light innumerable fires*
> *So that their neighbors in other cities*
> *Might see the glare reflected off the sky*
> *And sail to their help as allies in war.*                    225

So too the radiance that flared
From Achilles' head and up to the sky.
He went to the trench—away from the wall
And the other Greeks, out of respect
For his mother's tense command. Standing there,            230
He yelled, and behind him Pallas Athena
Amplified his voice, and shock waves
Reverberated through the Trojan ranks.

> *You have heard the piercing sound of horns*
> *When squadrons come to destroy a city.*                    235

The Greek's voice was like that,
Speaking bronze that made each Trojan heart
Wince with pain.
                        And the combed horses
Shied from their chariots, eyes wide with fear,            240
And their drivers went numb when they saw
The fire above Achilles' head
Burned into the sky by the Grey-Eyed One.
Three times Achilles shouted from the trench;
Three times the Trojans and their confederates            245
Staggered and reeled, twelve of their best
Lost in the crush of chariots and spears.
But the Greeks were glad to pull Patroclus' body
Out of range and placed it on a litter. His comrades
Gathered around, weeping, and with them Achilles,            250
Shedding hot tears when he saw his loyal friend

Stretched out on the litter, cut with sharp bronze.
He had sent him off to war with horses and chariot,
But he never welcomed him back home again.

And now the ox-eyed Lady Hera                           *255*
Sent the tireless, reluctant sun
Under the horizon into Ocean's streams,
Its last rays touching the departing Greeks with gold.
It had been a day of brutal warfare.

*[Lines 260–503 are omitted. The Trojans hold an assembly. Hector, reject-
ing the advice of his brother Polydamas, keeps the troops out on the plain.
The Greeks mourn Patroclus. Thetis goes to Hephaestus and asks him to
make a new set of armor for her son.]*

Hephaestus left her there and went to his bellows,
Turned them toward the fire and ordered them to work.    *505*
And the bellows, all twenty, blew on the crucibles,
Blasting out waves of heat in whatever direction
Hephaestus wanted as he hustled here and there
Around his forge and the work progressed.
He cast durable bronze onto the fire, and tin,           *510*
Precious gold and silver. Then he positioned
His enormous anvil up on its block
And grasped his mighty hammer
In one hand, and in the other his tongs.

He made a shield first, heavy and huge,                  *515*
Every inch of it intricately designed.
He threw a triple rim around it, glittering
Like lightning, and he made the strap silver.
The shield itself was five layers thick, and he
Crafted its surface with all of his genius.              *520*

> On it he made the earth, the sky, the sea,
> The unwearied sun, and the moon near full,
> And all the signs that garland the sky,
> Pleiades, Hyades, mighty Orion,

And the Bear they also call the Wagon,                              525
Which pivots in place and looks back at Orion
  And alone is aloof from the wash of Ocean.


  On it he made two cities, peopled
And beautiful. Weddings in one, festivals,
Brides led from their rooms by torchlight                           530
Up through the town, bridal song rising,
Young men reeling in dance to the tune
Of lyres and flutes, and the women
Standing in their doorways admiring them.
There was a crowd in the market-place                              535
And a quarrel arising between two men
Over blood money for a murder,
One claiming the right to make restitution,
The other refusing to accept any terms.
They were heading for an arbitrator                                 540
And the people were shouting, taking sides,
But heralds restrained them. The elders sat
On polished stone seats in the sacred circle
And held in their hands the staves of heralds.
The pair rushed up and pleaded their cases,                        545
And between them lay two ingots of gold
  For whoever spoke straightest in judgment.


  Around the other city two armies
Of glittering soldiery were encamped.
Their leaders were at odds–should they                             550
Move in for the kill or settle for a division
Of all the lovely wealth the citadel held fast?
The citizens wouldn't surrender, and armed
For an ambush. Their wives and little children
Were stationed on the wall, and with the old men                   555
Held it against attack. The citizens moved out,
Led by Ares and Pallas Athena,
Both of them gold, and their clothing was gold,
Beautiful and larger than life in their armor, as befits
Gods in their glory, and all the people were smaller.              560
They came to a position perfect for an ambush,

A spot on the river where stock came to water,
And took their places, concealed by fiery bronze.
Farther up they had two lookouts posted
Waiting to sight shambling cattle and sheep, 565
Which soon came along, trailed by two herdsmen
Playing their panpipes, completely unsuspecting.
When the townsmen lying in ambush saw this
They ran up, cut off the herds of cattle and fleecy
Silver sheep, and killed the two herdsmen. 570
When the armies sitting in council got wind
Of the ruckus with the cattle, they mounted
Their high-stepping horses and galloped to the scene.
They took their stand and fought along the river banks,
Throwing bronze-tipped javelins against each other. 575
Among them were Hate and Din and the Angel of Death,
Holding a man just wounded, another unwounded,
And dragging one dead by his heels from the fray,
And the cloak on her shoulders was red with human blood.
They swayed in battle and fought like living men, 580
    And each side salvaged the bodies of their dead.

    On it he put a soft field, rich farmland
Wide and thrice-tilled, with many plowmen
Driving their teams up and down rows.
Whenever they came to the end of the field 585
And turned, a man would run up and hand them
A cup of sweet wine. Then they turned again
Back up the furrow pushing on through deep soil
To reach the other end. The field was black
Behind them, just as if plowed, and yet 590
    It was gold, all gold, forged to a wonder.

    On it he put land sectioned off for a king,
Where reapers with sharp sickles were working.
Cut grain lay deep where it fell in the furrow,
And binders made sheaves bound with straw bands. 595
Three sheaf-binders stood by, and behind them children
Gathered up armfuls and kept passing them on.
The king stood in silence near the line of reapers,

Holding his staff, and his heart was happy.
Under an oaktree nearby heralds were busy                    *600*
Preparing a feast from an ox they had slaughtered
In sacrifice, and women were sprinkling it
    With abundant white barley for the reapers' dinner.


    On it he put a vineyard loaded with grapes,
Beautiful in gold. The clusters were dark,                   *605*
And the vines were set everywhere on silver poles.
Around it he inlaid a blue enamel ditch
And a fence of tin. A solitary path led to it,
And vintagers filed along it to harvest the grapes.
Girls, all grown up, and light-hearted boys                  *610*
Carried the honey-sweet fruit in wicker baskets.
Among them a boy picked out on a lyre
A beguiling tune and sang the Linos song
In a low, light voice, and the harvesters
    Skipped in time and shouted the refrain.                 *615*


    On it he made a herd of straight-horn cattle.
The cows were wrought of gold and tin
And rushed out mooing from the farmyard dung
To a pasture by the banks of a roaring river,
Making their way through swaying reeds.                      *620*
Four golden herdsmen tended the cattle,
And nine nimble dogs followed along.
Two terrifying lions at the front of the herd
Were pulling down an ox. Its long bellows alerted
The dogs and the lads, who were running on up,              *625*
But the two lions had ripped the bull's hide apart
And were gulping down the guts and black blood.
The shepherds kept trying to set on the dogs,
But they shied away from biting the lions
    And stood there barking just out of harm's way.         *630*


    On it the renowned lame god made a pasture
In a lovely valley, wide, with silvery sheep in it,
    And stables, roofed huts, and stone animal pens.

On it the renowned lame god embellished
A dancing ground, like the one Daedalus                    *635*
Made for ringleted Ariadne in wide Cnossus.
Young men and girls in the prime of their beauty
Were dancing there, hands clasped around wrists.
The girls wore delicate linens, and the men
Finespun tunics glistening softly with oil.                *640*
Flowers crowned the girls' heads, and the men
Had golden knives hung from silver straps.
They ran on feet that knew how to run
With the greatest ease, like a potter's wheel
When he stoops to cup it in the palms of his hands         *645*
And gives it a spin to see how it runs. Then they
Would run in lines that weaved in and out.
A large crowd stood round the beguiling dance,
Enjoying themselves, and two acrobats
    Somersaulted among them on cue to the music.          *650*


On it he put the great strength of the River Ocean,
Lapping the outermost rim of the massive shield.


And when he had wrought the shield, huge and heavy,
He made a breastplate gleaming brighter than fire
And a durable helmet that fit close at the temples,        *655*
Lovely and intricate, and crested with gold.
And he wrought leg-armor out of pliant tin.
And when the renowned lame god had finished this gear,
He set it down before Achilles' mother,
And she took off like a hawk from snow-capped Olympus,     *660*
Carrying armor through the sky like summer lightning.

# ILIAD 19

Dawn shrouded in saffron
Rose out of the deep water with light
For immortals and humans alike.
                                And Thetis
Came to the ships with Hephaestus' gifts.                    5
She found her son lying beside
His Patroclus, wailing,
And around him his many friends,
Mourning. The silvery goddess
Stood in their midst, took his hand,                         10
Whispered his name, and said to him:

"Achilles, you must let him rest,
No matter our grief. This man was gentled
By the gods. But you, my son, my darling,
Take this glorious armor from Hephaestus,                    15
So very beautiful, no man has ever worn
Anything like it."

                        She spoke,
And when she set the armor down before Achilles,
All of the metalwork clattered and chimed.                   20
The Myrmidons shuddered, and to a man
Could not bear to look at it. But Achilles,
When he saw it, felt his rage seep
Deeper into his bones, and his lids narrowed
And lowered over eyes that glared                            25
Like a white-hot steel flame. He turned
The polished weapons the god had given him
Over and over in his hands, and felt
Pangs of joy at all its intricate beauty.
And his words rose on wings                                  30
To meet his mother:

"My mother,
A god has given me these weapons–no
Mortal could have made them–and it is time
I arm myself in them. But I am afraid                         35
For Patroclus, afraid that flies
Will infest his wounds and breed worms
In his body, now the life is gone,
And his flesh turn foul and rotten."

The silver-footed goddess answered:                          40

"Do not let that trouble you, child.
I will protect him from the swarming flies
That infest humans slain in war.
Even if he should lie out for a full year
His flesh would still be as firm, or better.               45
But call an assembly now. Renounce
Your rage against Agamemnon.
Arm yourself for war and put on your strength."

Saying this, she multiplied his heroic temper.
Then she dripped ambrosia and ruby nectar                    50
Through Patroclus' nostrils, to keep his flesh firm.

And then Achilles went along the shore
Etched in sunlight, and shouted so loud
That not only the heroes came out, but all those too
Who had spent the war among the encamped ships,             55
All the pilots and oarsmen and stewards and cooks—
They all came to the assembly then, because Achilles,
Who had abstained a long time, was back.
Limping along were the two veterans,
Battle-scarred Diomedes and brilliant Odysseus,             60
Badly wounded, using their spears as crutches.
They came in and sat at the front of the assembly,
And behind them came the warlord, Agamemnon,
Wounded himself (that spear thrust by Coön,
Son of Antenor, in a hard-fought battle).                    65
When all of the Greeks were gathered together,

Swift-footed Achilles rose and addressed them:

"Well, son of Atreus, are either of us better off
For this anger that has eaten our hearts away
Like acid, this bitter quarrel over a girl?                                  70
Artemis should have shot her aboard my ship
The day I pillaged Lyrnessus and took her.
Far fewer Greeks would have gone down in the dust
Under Trojan hands, while I nursed my grudge.
Hector and the Trojans are better off. But the Greeks?      75
I think they will remember our quarrel forever.
But we'll let all that be, no matter how it hurts,
And conquer our pride, because we must.
I hereby end my anger. There is no need for me
To rage relentlessly. But let's move quickly now          80
To get our troops back into battle
So I can confront the Trojans and test their will
To bivouac among our ships. They will more likely
Be thankful to rest their knees at day's end,
If any of them gets out of this alive."                          85


He spoke, and the Greeks cheered.
Peleus' great son had renounced his rage.


[Lines 88–293 are omitted. Agamemnon and Achilles are reconciled.]


The assembly broke up and the men scattered,
Each to his own ship. The Myrmidons got busy          295
With the gifts, bringing them to Achilles' ship.
They stored it all in his huts, left the women there,
And proudly drove the horses to the herd.

Briseis stood there like golden Aphrodite.

But when she saw Patroclus' mangled body                300
She threw herself upon him and wailed
In a high, piercing voice, and with her nails
She tore her breast and soft neck and lovely face.

And this woman, so like a goddess, cried in anguish:

"My poor Patroclus. You were so dear to me.              *305*
When I left this hut you were alive,
And now I find you, the army's leader, dead
When I come back. So it is for me always,
Evil upon evil. I have seen my husband,
The man my father and mother gave me to,                  *310*
Mangled with sharp bronze before my city,
And my three brothers, all from the same mother,
Brothers I loved—they all died that day.
But you wouldn't let me cry when Achilles
Killed my husband and destroyed Mynes' city,             *315*
Wouldn't let me cry. You told me you'd make me
Achilles' bride, told me you'd take me on a ship
To Phthia, for a wedding among the Myrmidons.
I will never stop grieving for you, forever sweet."

Thus Briseis, and the women mourned with her,            *320*
For Patroclus, yes, but each woman also
For her own private sorrows.

               Around Achilles
The Achaean elders gathered, begging him to eat,
But he refused them, groaning:                            *325*

                  "I beg you, my friends—
Aren't any of you listening? Don't keep asking me
To satisfy my heart with food or drink
Before it is time. My grief is too great.
I will stay as I am and endure until sunset."             *330*

And he waved them off. Only Atreus' two sons
Remained with him, along with Odysseus,
Nestor, and the old charioteer, Phoenix,
Trying to comfort him in his grief's extremity.
But he could not be comforted. His heart would ache       *335*
Until he lost himself in war's blood-stained mouth.
Memories welled up and caught in his throat:

"There was a time, my ill-fated, beloved friend,
You would serve me a fine dinner in this hut,
Deftly and quickly, while the army hurried                          *340*
To bring war's sorrow to the horse-breaking Trojans.
Now you lie here a mangled corpse, and my heart
Fasts from the food and drink that are here
Out of grief for you. I could not suffer worse,
Not even if I learned my father were dead,                          *345*
Who perhaps is weeping back in Phthia right now
Because he misses his son who is off fighting
On Trojan soil—for Helen, at whom we all shudder.
Not even if it were my son, Neoptolemus,
Who is being reared for me in Scyrus, if indeed                     *350*
My dear child is still alive. I had hoped,
Until now, that I alone would perish at Troy,
And that you would return, and take my boy
In your swift black ship away from Scyrus
And show him all my things back home in Phthia.                     *355*
For Peleus by now must be dead and gone,
Or if he does still live he draws his breath in pain,
Clinging to a shred of life and always expecting
The grim message that will tell him I am dead."

He wept, and the elders added their laments to his,                 *360*
Each remembering what he had left at home.

Zeus saw them in their grief and, pitying them,
Spoke to Athena these feathered words:

"My child, have you deserted your warrior?
Do you no longer have any thought for Achilles?                     *365*
He is mourning his friend, sitting there
In front of his upswept hulls. Everyone else
Has gone off to dinner, but he refuses to eat.
Go drip some nectar and savory ambrosia
Into his breast, so he will not weaken with hunger."               *370*

Athena needed no encouragement. She flew
From the crystal sky like a shrill raptor

And pounced on Achilles. The other Achaeans
Were busy arming for battle. Athena distilled
Nectar and ambrosia into Achilles' chest 375
So that grim hunger would not weaken his knees,
And then was gone, back to her father's house,
While the Greeks poured out from their beached ships.

*Snow flurries can come so thick and fast*
*From the cold northern sky that the wind* 380
*That bears them becomes an icy, blinding glare.*

So too the gleaming, polished weaponry—
The helmets, shields, spears, and plated corselets—
All the bronze paraphernalia of war
That issued from the ships. The rising glare 385
Reflected off the coppery sky, and the land beneath
Laughed under the arcing metallic glow.
A deep bass thrumming rose from the marching feet.
And, like a bronze bolt in the center, Achilles,
Who now began to arm. 390
His eyes glowed
Like white-hot steel, and he gritted his teeth
Against the grief that had sunk into his bones,
And every motion he made in putting on the armor
Forged for him in heaven was an act of passion 395
Directed against the Trojans: clasping on his shins
The greaves trimmed in silver at the ankles,
Strapping the corselet onto his chest, slinging
The silver-studded bronze sword around a shoulder,
And then lifting the massive, heavy shield 400
That spilled light around it as if it were the moon.

*Or a fire that has flared up in a lonely settlement*
*High in the hills of an island, reflecting light*
*On the faces of men who have put out to sea*
*And must watch helplessly as rising winds* 405
*Bear them away from their dear ones.*

So too the terrible beauty of Achilles' shield,

A fire in the sky.
         He lifted the helmet
And placed it on his head, and it shone like a star,                    410
With the golden horsehair Hephaestus had set
Thickly on the crest rippling in waves.
He tested the fit and flex of the armor,
Sprinting on the sand, and found that the metal
Lifted him like wings. He pulled from its case                          415
His father's spear, the massive, heavy
Spear that only Achilles could handle,
Made of Pelian ash, which the centaur Chiron
Had brought down from Mount Pelion and given
To Achilles' father to be the death of heroes.                          420
Automedon and Alcimus harnessed the horses,
Cinched the leather straps, fit the bits in their jaws
And drew the reins back to the jointed chariot.
Automedon picked up the bright lash
And jumped into the car, and behind him                                 425
Achilles stepped in, shining in his war gear
Like an amber Sun, and in a cold voice
He cried to his father's horses:

"Xanthus and Balius, Podarge's famous colts,
See that you bring your charioteer back                                 430
Safe this time when we have had enough of war
And not leave him for dead, as you left Patroclus."

And from beneath the yoke Xanthus spoke back,
Hooves shimmering, his head bowed so low
That his mane swept the ground, as Hera,                                435
The white-armed goddess, gave him a voice:

"This time we will save you, mighty Achilles,
This time—but your hour is near. We
Are not to blame, but a great god and strong Fate.
Nor was it slowness or slackness on our part                           440
That allowed the Trojans to despoil Patroclus.
No, the best of gods, fair-haired Leto's son,
Killed him in the front lines and gave Hector the glory.

As for us, we could outrun the West Wind,
Which men say is the swiftest, but it is your destiny 445
To be overpowered by a mortal and a god."

Xanthus said this; then the Furies stopped his voice.
And Achilles, greatly troubled, answered him:

"I don't need you to prophesy my death,
Xanthus. I know in my bones I will die here 450
Far from my father and mother. Still, I won't stop
Until I have made the Trojans sick of war."

And with a cry he drove his horses to the front.

*[Books 20 and 21 are omitted. The gods join the battle. Achilles, looking for Hector, faces off with Aeneas, who is saved by Poseidon. Achilles then goes on a rampage, killing fourteen Trojans in quick succession. Hector at first avoids Achilles, but when Achilles kills his youngest brother, Polydorus, Hector faces Achilles. Apollo intervenes and saves Hector from Achilles' spear. Achilles presses on, killing Trojans mercilessly. The River Xanthus rises in rage against Achilles and nearly overwhelms him. Hera has Hephaestus fight the river with fire, and the river god begs for mercy. The gods battle each other. Achilles continues on to Troy. Apollo, disguised as a Trojan, acts as a decoy to lead Achilles away from the city while the Trojans retreat to within their walls.]*

# ILIAD 22

Everywhere you looked in Troy, exhausted
Soldiers, glazed with sweat like winded deer,
Leaned on the walls, cooling down
And slaking their thirst.
       Outside, the Greeks    *5*
Formed up close to the wall, locking their shields.
In the dead air between the Greeks
And Troy's Western Gate, Destiny
Had Hector pinned, waiting for death.

Then Apollo called back to Achilles:    *10*

"Son of Peleus, you're fast on your feet,
But you'll never catch me, man chasing god.
Or are you too raging mad to notice
I'm a god? Don't you care about fighting
The Trojans any more? You've chased them back    *15*
Into their town, but now you've veered off here.
You'll never kill me. You don't hold my doom."

And the shining sprinter, Achilles:

"That was a dirty trick, Apollo,
Turning me away from the wall like that!    *20*
I could have ground half of Troy face down
In the dirt! Now you've robbed me
Of my glory and saved them easily
Because you have no retribution to fear.
I swear, I'd make you pay if I could!"    *25*

His mind opened to the clear space before him,
And he was off toward the town, moving

  *Like a thoroughbred stretching it out*
  *Over the plain for the final sprint home—*

Achilles, lifting his knees as he lengthened his stride.  *30*

Priam saw him first, with his old man's eyes,
A single point of light on Troy's dusty plain.

> *Sirius rises late in the dark, liquid sky*
> *On summer nights, star of stars,*
> *Orion's Dog they call it, brightest*   *35*
> *Of all, but an evil portent, bringing heat*
> *And fevers to suffering humanity.*

Achilles' bronze gleamed like this as he ran.

And the old man groaned, and beat his head
With his hands, and stretched out his arms   *40*
To his beloved son, Hector, who had
Taken his stand before the Western Gate,
Determined to meet Achilles in combat.

Priam's voice cracked as he pleaded:

"Hector, my boy, you can't face Achilles   *45*
Alone like that, without any support—
You'll go down in a minute. He's too much
For you, son, he won't stop at anything!
O, if only the gods loved him as I do:
Vultures and dogs would be gnawing his corpse.   *50*
Then some grief might pass from my heart.
So many fine sons he's taken from me,
Killed or sold them as slaves in the islands.
Two of them now, Lycaon and Polydorus,
I can't see with the Trojans safe in town,   *55*
Laothoë's boys. If the Greeks have them
We'll ransom them with the gold and silver
Old Altes gave us. But if they're dead
And gone down to Hades, there will be grief
For myself and the mother who bore them.   *60*
The rest of the people won't mourn so much
Unless *you* go down at Achilles' hands.

So come inside the wall, my boy.
Live to save the men and women of Troy.
Don't just hand Achilles the glory                              *65*
And throw your life away. Show some pity for me
Before I go out of my mind with grief
And Zeus finally destroys me in my old age,
After I have seen all the horrors of war—
My sons butchered, my daughters dragged off,                   *70*
Raped, bedchambers plundered, infants
Dashed to the ground in this terrible war,
My sons' wives abused by murderous Greeks.
And one day some Greek soldier will stick me
With cold bronze and draw the life from my limbs,              *75*
And the dogs that I fed at my table,
My watchdogs, will drag me outside and eat
My flesh raw, crouched in my doorway, lapping
My blood.
               When a young man is killed in war,              *80*
Even though his body is slashed with bronze,
He lies there beautiful in death, noble.
But when the dogs maraud an old man's head,
Griming his white hair and beard and private parts,
There's no human fate more pitiable."                          *85*


And the old man pulled the white hair from his head,
But did not persuade Hector.


                              His mother then,
Wailing, sobbing, laid open her bosom
And holding out a breast spoke through her tears:              *90*


"Hector, my child, if ever I've soothed you
With this breast, remember it now, son, and
Have pity on me. Don't pit yourself
Against that madman. Come inside the wall.
If Achilles kills you I will never                             *95*
Get to mourn you laid out on a bier, O
My sweet blossom, nor will Andromache,
Your beautiful wife, but far from us both

Dogs will eat your body by the Greek ships."

So the two of them pleaded with their son,                    *100*
But did not persuade him or touch his heart.
Hector held his ground as Achilles' bulk
Loomed larger. He waited as a snake waits,

> *Tense and coiled*
> *As a man approaches*                                       *105*
> *Its lair in the mountains,*
> *Venom in its fangs*
> *And poison in its heart,*
> *Glittering eyes*
> *Glaring from the rocks:*                                   *110*

So Hector waited, leaning his polished shield
Against one of the towers in Troy's bulging wall,
But his heart was troubled with brooding thoughts:

"Now what? If I take cover inside,
Polydamas will be the first to reproach me.                   *115*
He begged me to lead the Trojans back
To the city on that black night when Achilles rose.
But I wouldn't listen, and now I've destroyed
Half the army through my recklessness.
I can't face the Trojan men and women now,                    *120*
Can't bear to hear some lesser man say,
'Hector trusted his strength and lost the army.'
That's what they'll say. I'll be much better off
Facing Achilles, either killing him
Or dying honorably before the city.                           *125*
    But what if I lay down all my weapons,
Bossed shield, heavy helmet, prop my spear
Against the wall, and go meet Achilles,
Promise him we'll surrender Helen
And everything Paris brought back with her                    *130*
In his ships' holds to Troy—that was the beginning
Of this war—give all of it back
To the sons of Atreus and divide

Everything else in the town with the Greeks,
And swear a great oath not to hold                                   *135*
Anything back, but share it all equally,
All the treasure in Troy's citadel.
   But why am I talking to myself like this?
I can't go out there unarmed. Achilles
Will cut me down in cold blood if I take off                         *140*
My armor and go out to meet him
Naked like a woman. This is no time
For talking, the way a boy and a girl
Whisper to each other from oak tree or rock,
A boy and a girl with all their sweet talk.                          *145*
Better to lock up in mortal combat
As soon as possible and see to whom
God on Olympus grants the victory."

Thus Hector.
          And Achilles closed in                *150*
Like the helmeted God of War himself,
The ash-wood spear above his right shoulder
Rocking in the light that played from his bronze
In gleams of fire and the rising sun.
And when Hector saw it he lost his nerve,                            *155*
Panicked, and ran, leaving the gates behind,
With Achilles on his tail, confident in his speed.

   *You have seen a falcon*
   *In a long, smooth dive*
   *Attack a fluttering dove*                                 *160*
   *Far below in the hills.*
   *The falcon screams,*
   *Swoops, and plunges*
   *In its lust for prey.*

So Achilles swooped and Hector trembled                              *165*
In the shadow of Troy's wall.
                Running hard,
They passed Lookout Rock and the windy fig tree,
Following the loop of the wagon road.

They came to the wellsprings of eddying                    *170*
Scamander, two beautiful pools, one
Boiling hot with steam rising up,
The other flowing cold even in summer,
Cold as freezing sleet, cold as tundra snow.
There were broad basins there, lined with stone,           *175*
Where the Trojan women used to wash their silky clothes
In the days of peace, before the Greeks came.

They ran by these springs, pursuer and pursued—
A great man out front, a far greater behind—
And they ran all out. This was not a race                  *180*
For such a prize as athletes compete for,
An oxhide or animal for sacrifice, but a race
For the lifeblood of Hector, breaker of horses.

> *But champion horses wheeling round the course,*
> *Hooves flying, pouring it on in a race for a prize—*     *185*
> *A woman or tripod—at a hero's funeral games*

Will give you some idea of how these heroes looked
As they circled Priam's town three times running
    While all the gods looked on.

Zeus, the gods' father and ours, spoke:                    *190*

"I do not like what I see, a man close
To my heart chased down around Troy's wall.
Hector has burned many an ox's thigh
To me, both on Ida's peaks and in the city's
High holy places, and now Achilles                         *195*
Is running him down around Priam's town.
Think you now, gods, and take counsel whether
We should save him from death or deliver him
Into Achilles' hands, good man though he be."

The grey-eyed goddess Athena answered:                     *200*

    "O Father,
You may be the Lord of Lightning and the Dark Cloud,

But what a thing to say, to save a mortal man,
With his fate already fixed, from rattling death!
Do it. But don't expect us all to approve."                    *205*

Zeus loomed like a thunderhead, but answered gently:

"There, there, daughter, my heart wasn't in it.
I did not mean to displease you, my child. Go now,
Do what you have in mind without delay."

Athena had been longing for action                              *210*
And at his word shot down from Olympus,
As Achilles bore down on Hector.

    *A hunting hound starts a fawn in the hills,*
    *Follows it through brakes and hollows,*
    *And if it hides in a thicket, circles,*             *215*
    *Picks up the trail, and renews the chase.*

No more could Hector elude Achilles.
Every time Hector surged for the Western Gate
Under the massive towers, hoping for
Trojan archers to give him some cover,                          *220*
Achilles cut him off and turned him back
Toward the plain, keeping the inside track.

    *Running in a dream, you can't catch up,*
    *You can't catch up and you can't get away.*

No more could Achilles catch Hector                             *225*
Or Hector escape.
               And how could Hector
Have ever escaped death's black birds
If Apollo had not stood by his side
This one last time and put life in his knees?                  *230*

Achilles shook his head at his soldiers:
He would not allow anyone to shoot
At Hector and win glory with a hit,
Leaving him only to finish him off.

But when they reached the springs the fourth time,                235
Father Zeus stretched out his golden scales
And placed on them two agonizing deaths,
One for Achilles and one for Hector.
When he held the beam, Hector's doom sank down
Toward Hades. And Phoebus Apollo left him.                         240

By now the grey-eyed goddess Athena
Was at Achilles' side, and her words flew fast:

"There's nothing but glory on the beachhead
For us now, my splendid Achilles,
Once we take Hector out of action, and                            245
There's no way he can escape us now,
Not even if my brother Apollo has a fit
And rolls on the ground before the Almighty.
You stay here and catch your breath while I go
To persuade the man to put up a fight."                           250

Welcome words for Achilles. He rested,
Leaning on his heavy ash and bronze spear,
While the goddess made her way to Hector,
The spitting image of Deïphobus.
And her voice sounded like his as she said:                       255

"Achilles is pushing you hard, brother,
In this long footrace around Priam's town.
Why don't we stand here and give him a fight?"

Hector's helmet flashed as he turned and said:

"Deïphobus, you've always been my favorite                        260
Brother, and again you've shown me why,
Having the courage to come out for me,
Leaving the safety of the wall, while all
Priam's other sons are cowering inside."

And Athena, her eyes as grey as winter moons:                     265

"Mother and father begged me by my knees
To stay inside, and so did all my friends.
That's how frightened they are, Hector. But I
Could not bear the pain in my heart, brother.
Now let's get tough and fight and not spare                    270
Any spears. Either Achilles kills us both
And drags our blood-soaked gear to the ships,
Or he goes down with your spear in his guts."

That's how Athena led him on, with guile.
And when the two heroes faced each other,                      275
Great Hector, helmet shining, spoke first:

"I'm not running any more, Achilles.
Three times around the city was enough.
I've got my nerve back. It's me or you now.
But first we should swear a solemn oath.                       280
With all the gods as witnesses, I swear:
If Zeus gives me the victory over you,
I will not dishonor your corpse, only
Strip the armor and give the body back
To the Greeks. Promise you'll do the same."                   285

And Achilles, fixing his eyes on him:

"Don't try to cut any deals with me, Hector.
Do lions make peace treaties with men?
Do wolves and lambs agree to get along?
No, they hate each other to the core,                         290
And that's how it is between you and me,
No talk of agreements until one of us
Falls and gluts Ares with his blood.
By God, you'd better remember everything
You ever knew about fighting with spears.                     295
But you're as good as dead. Pallas Athena
And my spear will make you pay in a lump
For the agony you've caused by killing my friends."

With that he pumped his spear arm and let fly.
Hector saw the long flare the javelin made, and ducked.       300

The bronze point sheared the air over his head
And rammed into the earth. But Athena
Pulled it out and gave it back to Achilles
Without Hector noticing. And Hector,
Prince of Troy, taunted Achilles: 305

"Ha! You missed! Godlike Achilles! It looks like
You didn't have my number after all.
You said you did, but you were just trying
To scare me with big words and empty talk.
Did you think I'd run and you'd plant a spear 310
In my back? It'll take a direct hit in my chest,
Coming right at you, that and a god's help too.
Now see if you can dodge this piece of bronze.
Swallow it whole! The war will be much easier
On the Trojans with you dead and gone." 315

And Hector let his heavy javelin fly,
A good throw, too, hitting Achilles' shield
Dead center, but it only rebounded away.
Angry that his throw was wasted, Hector
Fumbled about for a moment, reaching 320
For another spear. He shouted to Deïphobus,
But Deïphobus was nowhere in sight.
It was then that Hector knew in his heart
What had happened, and said to himself:

"I hear the gods calling me to my death. 325
I thought I had a good man here with me,
Deïphobus, but he's still on the wall.
Athena tricked me. Death is closing in
And there's no escape. Zeus and Apollo
Must have chosen this long ago, even though 330
They used to be on my side. Well, this is fate,
But I will not perish without doing some great deed
That future generations will remember."

And he drew the sharp broadsword that hung
By his side and gathered himself for a charge. 335

*A high-flying eagle dives*
*Through ebony clouds down*
*To the sun-scutched plain to claw*
*A lamb or a quivering hare.*

Thus Hector's charge, and the light                    340
That played from his blade's honed edge.

Opposite him, Achilles exploded forward, fury
Incarnate behind the curve of his shield,
A glory of metalwork, and the plumes
Nodded and rippled on his helmet's crest,                    345
Thick golden horsehair set by Hephaestus,
And his spearpoint glinted like the Evening Star

*In the gloom of night,*
*Star of perfect splendor,*

A gleam in the air as Achilles poised                    350
His spear with murderous aim at Hector,
Eyes boring into the beautiful skin,
Searching for the weak spot. Hector's body
Was encased in the glowing bronze armor
He had stripped from the fallen Patroclus,                    355
But where the collarbones join at the neck
The gullet offered swift and certain death.
It was there Achilles drove his spear through
As Hector charged. The heavy bronze apex
Pierced the soft neck but did not slit the windpipe,                    360
So that Hector could speak still.
He fell back in the dust.

And Achilles exulted:

"So you thought you could get away with it
Didn't you, Hector? Killing Patroclus                    365
And ripping off his armor, *my* armor,
Thinking I was too far away to matter.
You fool. His avenger was far greater—

And far closer—than you could imagine,
Biding his time back in our beachhead camp.                    *370*
And now I have laid you out on the ground.
Dogs and birds are going to draw out your guts
While the Greeks give Patroclus burial."

And Hector, barely able to shake the words out:

"I beg you, Achilles, by your own soul                         *375*
And by your parents, do not
Allow the dogs to mutilate my body
By the Greek ships. Accept the gold and bronze
Ransom my father and mother will give you
And send my body back home to be burned                        *380*
In honor by the Trojans and their wives."

And Achilles, fixing him with a stare:

"Don't whine to me about my parents,
You dog! I wish my stomach would let me
Cut off your flesh in strips and eat it raw                    *385*
For what you've done to me. There is no one
And no way to keep the dogs off your head,
Not even if they bring ten or twenty
Ransoms, pile them up here and promise more,
Not even if Dardanian Priam weighs your body                   *390*
Out in gold, not even then will your mother
Ever get to mourn you laid out on a bier.
No, dogs and birds will eat every last scrap."

Helmet shining, Hector spoke his last words:

"So this is Achilles. There was no way                         *395*
To persuade you. Your heart is a lump
Of iron. But the gods will not forget this,
And I will have my vengeance on that day
When Paris and Apollo destroy you
In the long shadow of Troy's Western Gate."                    *400*

Death's veil covered him as he said these things,
And his soul, bound for Hades, fluttered out
Resentfully, forsaking manhood's bloom.

He was dead when Achilles spoke to him:

"Die and be done with it. As for my fate,                    405
I'll accept it whenever Zeus sends it."

And he drew the bronze spear out of the corpse,
Laid it aside, then stripped off the blood-stained armor.
The other Greeks crowded around
And could not help but admire Hector's                       410
Beautiful body, but still they stood there
Stabbing their spears into him, smirking.

"Hector's a lot softer to the touch now
Than he was when he was burning our ships,"

One of them would say, pulling out his spear.               415

After Achilles had stripped the body
He rose like a god and addressed the Greeks:

"Friends, Argive commanders and counsellors,
The gods have granted us this man's defeat,
Who did us more harm than all the rest                      420
Put together. What do you say we try
Laying a close siege on the city now
So we can see what the Trojans intend—
Whether they will give up the citadel
With Hector dead, or resolve to fight on?                    425
    But what am I thinking of? Patroclus' body
Still lies by the ships, unmourned, unburied,
Patroclus, whom I will never forget
As long as I am among the living,
Until I rise no more; and even if                            430
In Hades the dead do not remember,
Even there I will remember my dear friend.

   Now let us chant the victory paean, sons
Of the Achaeans, and march back to our ships
With this hero in tow. The power and the glory                    *435*
Are ours. We have killed great Hector,
Whom all the Trojans honored as a god."

But it was shame and defilement Achilles
Had in mind for Hector. He pierced the tendons
Above the heels and cinched them with leather thongs              *440*
To his chariot, letting Hector's head drag.
He mounted, hoisted up the prize armor,
And whipped his team to a willing gallop
Across the plain. A cloud of dust rose
Where Hector was hauled, and the long black hair                  *445*
Fanned out from his head, so beautiful once,
As it trailed in the dust. In this way Zeus
Delivered Hector into his enemies' hands
To be defiled in his own native land.

Watching this from the wall, Hector's mother                      *450*
Tore off her shining veil and screamed,
And his old father groaned pitifully,
And all through town the people were convulsed
With lamentation, as if Troy itself,
The whole towering city, were in flames.                          *455*
They were barely able to restrain
The old man, frantic to run through the gates,
Imploring them all, rolling in the dung,
And finally making this desperate appeal:

"Please let me go, alone, to the Greek ships.                     *460*
I don't care if you're worried. I want to see
If that monster will respect my age, pity me
For the sake of his own father, Peleus,
Who is about my age, old Peleus
Who bore him and bred him to be a curse                           *465*
For the Trojans, but he's caused me more pain
Than anyone, so many of my sons,
Beautiful boys, he's killed. I miss them all,

But I miss Hector more than all of them.
My grief for him will lay me in the earth.          470
Hector! You should have died in my arms, son!
Then we could have satisfied our sorrow,
Mourning and weeping, your mother and I."

The townsmen moaned as Priam was speaking.
Then Hecuba raised the women's lament:          475

"Hector, my son, I am desolate!
How can I live with suffering like this,
With you dead? You were the only comfort
I had, day and night, wherever you were
In the town, and you were the only hope          480
For Troy's men and women. They honored you
As a god when you were alive, Hector.
Now death and doom have overtaken you."

   And all this time Andromache had heard
Nothing about Hector—news had not reached her          485
That her husband was caught outside the walls.
She was working the loom in an alcove
Of the great hall, embroidering flowers
Into a purple cloak, and had just called
To her serving women, ordering them          490
To put a large cauldron on the fire, so
A steaming bath would be ready for Hector
When he came home from battle. Poor woman,
She had little idea how far from warm baths
Hector was, undone by the Grey-Eyed One          495
And delivered into the hands of the Greeks.

Then she heard the lamentation from the tower.

She trembled, and the shuttle fell
To the floor. Again she called her women:

"Two of you come with me. I must see          500
What has happened. That was Hecuba's voice.

My heart is in my throat, my knees are like ice.
Something terrible has happened to one
Of Priam's sons. O God, I'm afraid
Achilles has cut off my brave Hector     *505*
Alone on the plain outside the city
And has put an end to my husband's
Cruel courage. Hector never held back
Safe in the ranks; he always charged ahead,
Second to no one in fighting spirit."     *510*

With these words on her lips Andromache
Ran outdoors like a madwoman, heart racing,
Her two waiting-women following behind.
She reached the tower, pushed through the crowd,
And looking out from the wall saw her husband     *515*
As the horses dragged him disdainfully
Away from the city to the hollow Greek ships.

Black night swept over her eyes.
She reeled backward, gasping, and her veil
And glittering headbands flew off,     *520*
The diadem golden Aphrodite
Gave her on that day when tall-helmed Hector
Led her from her father's house in marriage.
And now her womenfolk were around her,
Hector's sisters and his brother's wives,     *525*
Holding her as she raved madly for death,
Until she caught her breath and her distraught
Spirit returned to her breast. She moaned then
And, surrounded by Trojan women, spoke:

"Hector, you and I have come to the grief     *530*
We were both born for, you in Priam's Troy
And I in Thebes in the house of Eïtion
Who raised me there beneath wooded Plakos
Under an evil star. Better never to have been born.
And now you are going to Hades' dark world,     *535*
Underground, leaving me in sorrow,
A widow in the halls, with an infant,

The son you and I bore but cannot bless.
You can't help him now you are dead, Hector,
And he can never help you. Even if                          540
He lives through this unbearable war,
There's nothing left for him in life but pain
And deprivation, all his property
Lost to others. An orphan has no friends.
He hangs his head, his cheeks are wet with tears.          545
He has to beg from his dead father's friends,
Tugging on one man's cloak, another's tunic,
And if they pity him he gets to sip
From someone's cup, just enough to moisten
His lips but not enough to quench his thirst.              550
Or a child with both parents still alive
Will push him away from a feast, taunting him,
'Go away, your father doesn't eat with us.'
And the boy will go to his widowed mother
In tears, Astyanax, who used to sit                        555
In his father's lap and eat nothing but
Mutton and marrow. When he got sleepy
And tired of playing he would take a nap
In a soft bed nestled in his nurse's arms
His dreaming head filled with blossoming joy.             560
But now he'll suffer, now he's lost his father.
The Trojans called him Astyanax
Because you alone were Troy's defender,
You alone protected their walls and gates.
Now you lie by the curved prows of the ships,            565
Far from your parents. The dogs will glut
On your naked body, and shiny maggots
Will eat what's left.
                         Your clothes are stored away,
Beautiful, fine clothes made by women's hands—           570
I'll burn them all now in a blazing fire.
They're no use to you, you'll never lie
On the pyre in them. Burning them will be
Your glory before Trojan men and women."


And the women's moans came in over her lament.           575

# ILIAD 23

While the Trojans lamented throughout the city,
The Greeks came to their beachhead camp
On the Hellespont and dispersed, each man
To his own ship.
                        But Achilles                                    5
Did not dismiss the Myrmidons.
He addressed his troops, men who lived for war:

"Myrmidons! I know you love your horses,
But before we unhitch them from the chariots
Let us all stay in armor and drive up close                            10
And weep for Patroclus. We owe it to the dead.
After we've indulged in grief and sorrow
We can loosen our horses and eat together."

He spoke, and led them in their lamentation.
Three times they drove their horses round the corpse,                  15
Wailing as they went. Thetis was with them,
And she honed their desire for grief. The sand
Was wet, and the warriors' armor, wet with tears.
They missed him. God, how he could fight!
Achilles' voice rose through their choked sobbing,                     20
As he placed his man-slaying hands on his friend's breast:

"I hail you, Patroclus, even in Hades!
I am fulfilling all that I promised before,
To drag Hector here and feed him raw to the dogs,
And to cut the throats of twelve fine Trojan boys                      25
Before your pyre, in my rage at your murder."

He spoke, and treated glorious Hector foully,
Stretching him out in the dust before the bier
Of Menoetius' son.

The men took off their armor,            30
Bronze gleaming in the dusk, and unhitched
Their whinnying horses, and sat down by the ship
Of Aeacus' swift grandson, too many to count.
And he made a funeral feast to satisfy their hearts.
Many sleek bulls bellowed beneath the knife            35
As they were slaughtered, many sheep, bleating goats,
And white-tusked boars, rich with fat,
Were skewered to roast over the fire's flame.
The ground around the corpse ran cup-deep with blood.

The other Greek leaders had come for Achilles            40
And were now escorting him to Agamemnon.
It had not been easy to convince him to come—
His heart raged for his friend. When they reached
Agamemnon's hut, they ordered the heralds
To put a cauldron on the fire, hoping to persuade            45
Achilles to bathe and wash off the gore.
He refused outright and swore this oath:

"By Zeus on high, there will not be
Any washing of my head until I have laid
Patroclus on the fire, and heaped his barrow,            50
And shorn my hair, for never will I grieve
Like this again, while I am among the living.
Now let's force ourselves to eat this feast.
But at the break of dawn, Agamemnon,
Order your men to bring wood and make ready            55
All that is fit for a dead man to have
When he goes beneath the murky gloom,
So that the fire may burn him quickly out of sight
And the men return to what they have to do."

He spoke, they listened, and they did as he said.            60
They prepared a meal and each man feasted,
And when they all had enough of food and drink,
They went to their huts and took their rest.
But the son of Peleus lay groaning heavily
Among his Myrmidons on the open beach            65

Where the waves crashed and seethed.
When sleep finally took him, unknotting his heart
And enveloping his shining limbs—so fatigued
From chasing Hector to windy Ilion—
Patroclus' sad spirit came, with his same form                              70
And with his beautiful eyes and his voice
And wearing the same clothes. He stood
Above Achilles' head, and said to him:

"You're asleep and have forgotten me, Achilles.
You never neglected me when I was alive,                                    75
But now, when I am dead! Bury me quickly
So I may pass through Hades' gates.
The spirits keep me at a distance, the phantoms
Of men outworn, and will not yet allow me
To join them beyond the River. I wander                                     80
Aimlessly through Hades' wide-doored house.
And give me your hand, for never again
Will I come back from Hades, once you burn me
In my share of fire. Never more in life
Shall we sit apart from our comrades and talk.                              85
The Fate I was born to has swallowed me,
And it is your destiny, though you are like the gods,
Achilles, to die beneath the wall of Troy.
And one thing more, Achilles. Do not lay my bones
Apart from yours, but let them lie together,                                90
Just as we were reared together in your house
After Menoetius brought me, still just a boy,
From Opoeis to your land because I had killed
Amphidamas' son on that day we played dice
And I foolishly became angry. I didn't mean to.                             95
Peleus took me into his house then and reared me
With kindness, and he named me your comrade.
So let one coffer enfold the bones of us both,
The two-handled gold one your mother gave you."

And Achilles answered him, saying:                                         100

"Why have you come to me here, dear heart,

With all these instructions? I promise you
I will do everything just as you ask.
But come closer. Let us give in to grief,
However briefly, in each other's arms."                    105

Saying this, Achilles reached out with his hands
But could not touch him. His spirit vanished like smoke,
Gone under the earth, with a last, shrill cry.
Awestruck, Achilles leapt up, clapping
His palms together, and said lamenting:                    110

"Ah, so there is something in Death's house,
A phantom spirit, although not in a body.
All night long poor Patroclus' spirit
Stood over me, weeping and wailing,
And giving me detailed instructions                        115
About everything. He looked so like himself."

His words aroused in them a longing for grief,
And they were still wailing around the corpse
When Dawn's roselight touched them.

                         Then Lord Agamemnon          120
Sent out from all over the camp a contingent
Of mules and men to gather wood,
Putting a good man in charge, Meriones,
Idomeneus' henchman. The men went out
With axes and ropes, and the mules before them,           125
Upward, downward, sideways, and slantwise,
Until they came to the spurs of spring-dotted Ida.
There they set to work felling high-crowned oaks
With bronze axes. The trees kept crashing down.
They split the trunks and bound them together             130
Behind the mules, who tore up the ground
As they tramped through underbrush toward the plain.
Meriones ordered the whole crew of woodcutters
To carry back logs, and they cast them down
On the shore in order, where Achilles planned             135
A great mound for Patroclus and for himself.

When they had laid out an immense amount of wood,
The crowd sat down and waited. Then Achilles
Ordered the Myrmidons to put on their armor
And yoke the horses to the chariots. They armed          140
And mounted, charioteers and warriors both,
And the chariots rolled out, with foot soldiers
Following behind in an endless cloud.
In the middle his comrades bore Patroclus,
Covering his body, as if with a garment,                 145
With hair they sheared off and cast upon it.
Behind them Achilles cradled his head, grieving
For the peerless friend he was sending to Hades.

When they came to the place Achilles had told them,
They put the body down and quickly heaped up             150
Enough wood and plenty. Then Achilles,
Acting on impulse, stood apart from the pyre
And sheared off his hair, the tawny hair
He had been growing long for the River Spercheius.
Brooding, he turned toward the open sea,                  155
The water glinting like wine, and said:

"Spercheius, my father Peleus vowed in vain
That when I had come home to my native land
I would shear my hair for you and sacrifice
Bulls by the hundred and fifty rams unblemished          160
Into your springs, where your precinct is
And your smoking altar. An old man's prayer,
Which you did not fulfill. Since I will never
Return home to my native land, I would give
To the hero Patroclus this lock to bear with him."       165

And he placed it in his beloved friend's hands.
This started them all weeping, and the sun
Would have set on their lamentation
Had not Achilles said to Agamemnon:

"Son of Atreus—you have the widest command—              170
These men can mourn all they want, but for now

Disperse them from the pyre and have them
Prepare their dinner. Those of us who are
Closest to the dead will do everything here.
And we would have all the leaders stay too."                175

The warlord Agamemnon heard him
And dismissed the troops to the ships.
The funeral party stayed and heaped up wood,
Building a pyre a hundred feet on each side,
And with heavy hearts they set the corpse on top.          180
Then they flayed many fine sheep and oxen
And laid them dressed out before the pyre.
Achilles gathered the fat from them all
And enfolded the body from head to foot,
Then heaped around it the flayed carcasses.                185
Next he set amphoras of honey and oil
Against the bier, and with heavy groans
Quickly cast on the pyre four high-necked horses.
Nine dogs once fed under the prince's table.
Achilles cut the throats of two and cast them on,          190
And twelve Trojans also, sons from good families,
Slashing them with bronze in a vengeful spirit.
Then he kindled the fire and let its iron will rage.
With a groan he called his beloved friend's name:

"Hear me, Patroclus, even from Hades.                       195
All that I promised you I am completing now.
Twelve Trojans, sons of good families,
The fire consumes with you. Hector, though,
I will not give to the fire to eat, but to dogs."

Thus went his threat, but no dogs would eat Hector.        200
Aphrodite kept the dogs from his corpse
By day and by night, and she anointed him
With ambrosial oil of rose, so that when Achilles
Dragged his body it would not be torn.
And Phoebus Apollo drew a dark blue cloud                   205
From the sky to the plain, covering the spot
Where the body lay, so that the sun's heat

Would not shrivel the flesh on his bones.

But Patroclus' pyre would not kindle.
Achilles thought of something else to try.                    *210*
Standing apart from the pyre, he prayed
To the North Wind and West Wind, promising
Fine offerings, pouring libations from a gold cup,
And earnestly beseeching them to come and blow
So the wood would kindle and the body burn.                   *215*
Iris heard his prayer and was off to the Winds
With the message. They were all in the house
Of the brisk West Wind, eating a banquet,
And Iris swooped to a stop on the stone threshold.
When they saw her there, they all whooshed up,                *220*
And each Wind invited her to sit next to him.
But she refused to sit, and made this speech:

"No seat for me. I'm off to Ocean's streams,
To the Ethiopians. They are offering sacrifices
To the immortals, and I want to get my share.                 *225*
But Achilles is praying for the Winds to come—
The North Wind and the howling West—
And he is promising fine offerings
If you will raise the fire on Patroclus' pyre,
For whom all the Achaeans are groaning aloud."                *230*

She spoke and was gone. And the Winds rose
With an eerie noise, driving clouds before them.
They reached the sea quickly, and the waves swelled
Under their whistling blast. When they came to Troy
They fell on the pyre, and the flames roared to life.         *235*
The whole night long the shrill winds blew steadily
On the funeral fire, and all the long night Achilles
Drew wine from a golden bowl and poured it out
From a two-handled cup, wetting the earth,
Ever summoning the spirit of forlorn Patroclus.               *240*

   *A father wails for his son as he burns*
   *His bones, a son newly wed, a son whose death*

*Has brought his parents inconsolable grief.*

Achilles wailed for his friend as he burned his bones,
Moving slowly about the pyre, groaning heavily.                     *245*

   The morning star rose, speaking light to the earth,
And dawn opened over the sea like a crocus.
The flames died down and the fire subsided.
The Winds left and returned to their home
Over the Thracian sea, and it moaned beneath them.                  *250*
Then the son of Peleus left the pyre
And lay down exhausted. He was soon asleep,
But the men with Agamemnon gathered around,
And the sound of their tramping woke him.
He sat up and spoke to them, saying:                                *255*

"Son of Atreus and princes of Greece,
First quench the funeral fire with wine,
Wherever it burned. Then gather the bones
Of Patroclus, son of Menoetius. Pick them out
Carefully. They are easily recognized,                              *260*
For he lay in the middle, while the others burned
Off to the sides, men and horses jumbled.
Then let us wrap the bones in fat and keep them
In a golden bowl, until I am hidden in Hades.
You need not labor over a huge barrow for him,                      *265*
But only what is seemly. Later the Achaeans
Can build it broad and high, all of you still left
Amid our thwarted ships when I am gone."

Thus Peleus' swift son, and they obeyed him.
First they doused the pyre with wine                                *270*
Wherever it had burned and the embers were thick.
Then they gathered the bones of their gentle comrade
Into a golden bowl, wrapping them twice in fat,
And they placed the bowl in the hut and covered it
With a soft linen cloth. Then they traced a circle                  *275*
For a mound and laid a foundation around the pyre
And piled up earth to form a tumulus over it.

Then they started to go back. But Achilles
Kept all the people there and had them sit down.
Then he brought prizes from his ship:                    *280*
Cauldrons, tripods, horses, mules, oxen,
Silken-waisted women, and grey iron.

*[The rest of Book 23 (lines 283–923) is omitted. Achilles hosts funeral games for Patroclus.]*

# ILIAD 24

*[Lines 1–496 are omitted. Achilles continues to desecrate Hector's body, which is preserved by Apollo. Apollo convinces the other gods to order Achilles to allow the body to be ransomed. Thetis goes to Achilles and persuades him to do so. Iris tells Priam to go to Achilles with ransom. Priam is guided by Hermes to Achilles' hut.]*

And with that Hermes left and returned
To high Olympus. Priam jumped down
And left Idaeus to hold the horses and mules.
The old man went straight to the house                    *500*
Where Achilles, dear to Zeus, sat and waited.

He found him inside. His companions sat
Apart from him, and a solitary pair,
Automedon and Alcimus, warriors both,
Were busy at his side. He had just finished                    *505*
His evening meal. The table was still set up.
Great Priam entered unnoticed. He stood
Close to Achilles, and touching his knees,
He kissed the dread and murderous hands
That had killed so many of his sons.                    *510*

*Passion sometimes blinds a man so completely*
*That he kills one of his own countrymen.*
*In exile, he comes into a wealthy house,*
*And everyone stares at him with wonder.*

So Achilles stared in wonder at Priam.                                    515
Was he a god?
                    And the others there stared
And wondered and looked at each other.
But Priam spoke, a prayer of entreaty:

"Remember your father, godlike Achilles.                                  520
He and I both are on the doorstep
Of old age. He may well be now
Surrounded by enemies wearing him down
And have no one to protect him from harm.
But then he hears that you are still alive                                525
And his heart rejoices, and he hopes all his days
To see his dear son come back from Troy.
But what is left for me? I had the finest sons
In all wide Troy, and not one of them is left.
Fifty I had when the Greeks came over,                                    530
Nineteen out of one belly, and the rest
The women in my house bore to me.
It doesn't matter how many they were,
The god of war has cut them down at the knees.
And the only one who could save the city                                  535
You've just now killed as he fought for his country,
My Hector. It is for him I have come to the Greek ships,
To get him back from you. I've brought
A fortune in ransom. Respect the gods, Achilles.
Think of your own father, and pity me.                                    540
I am more pitiable. I have borne what no man
Who has walked this earth has ever yet borne.
I have kissed the hand of the man who killed my son."

He spoke, and sorrow for his own father
Welled up in Achilles. He took Priam's hand                              545
And gently pushed the old man away.

The two of them remembered. Priam,
Huddled in grief at Achilles' feet, cried
And moaned softly for his man-slaying Hector.
And Achilles cried for his father and                           550
For Patroclus. The sound filled the room.

When Achilles had his fill of grief
And the aching sorrow left his heart,
He rose from his chair and lifted the old man
By his hand, pitying his white hair and beard.                  555
And his words enfolded him like wings:

"Ah, the suffering you've had, and the courage.
To come here alone to the Greek ships
And meet my eye, the man who slaughtered
Your many fine sons! You have a heart of iron.                  560
But come, sit on this chair. Let our pain
Lie at rest a while, no matter how much we hurt.
There's nothing to be gained from cold grief.
Yes, the gods have woven pain into mortal lives,
While they are free from care.                                  565
                        Two jars
Sit at the doorstep of Zeus, filled with gifts
That he gives, one full of good things,
The other of evil. If Zeus gives a man
A mixture from both jars, sometimes                             570
Life is good for him, sometimes not.
But if all he gives you is from the jar of woe,
You become a pariah, and hunger drives you
Over the bright earth, dishonored by gods and men.
Now take Peleus. The gods gave him splendid gifts               575
From the day he was born. He was the happiest
And richest man on earth, king of the Myrmidons,
And although he was a mortal, the gods gave him
An immortal goddess to be his wife.
But even to Peleus the god gave some evil:                      580
He would not leave offspring to succeed him in power,
Just one child, all out of season. I can't be with him
To take care of him now that he's old, since I'm far

From my fatherland, squatting here in Troy,
Tormenting you and your children. And you, old sir,                585
We hear that you were prosperous once.
From Lesbos down south clear over to Phrygia
And up to the Hellespont's boundary,
No one could match you in wealth or in sons.
But then the gods have brought you trouble,                590
This constant fighting and killing around your town.
You must endure this grief and not constantly grieve.
You will not gain anything by torturing yourself
Over the good son you lost, not bring him back.
Sooner you will suffer some other sorrow."                595

And Priam, old and godlike, answered him:

"Don't sit me in a chair, prince, while Hector
Lies uncared for in your hut. Deliver him now
So I can see him with my own eyes, and you—
Take all this ransom we bring, take pleasure in it,                600
And go back home to your own fatherland,
Since you've taken this first step and allowed me
To live and see the light of day."

Achilles glowered at him and said:

"Don't provoke me, old man. It's my own decision                605
To release Hector to you. A messenger came to me
From Zeus—my own natural mother,
Daughter of the old sea god. And I know you,
Priam, inside out. You don't fool me one bit.
Some god escorted you to the Greek ships.                610
No mortal would have dared come into our camp,
Not even your best young hero. He couldn't have
Gotten past the guards or muscled open the gate.
So just stop stirring up grief in my heart,
Or I might not let you out of here alive, old man—                615
Suppliant though you are—and sin against Zeus."

The old man was afraid and did as he was told.

The son of Peleus leapt out the door like a lion,
Followed by Automedon and Alcimus, whom Achilles
Honored most now that Patroclus was dead. 620
They unyoked the horses and mules, and led
The old man's herald inside and seated him on a chair.
Then they unloaded from the strong-wheeled cart
The endless ransom that was Hector's blood price,
Leaving behind two robes and a finespun tunic 625
For the body to be wrapped in and brought inside.
Achilles called the women and ordered them
To wash the body well and anoint it with oil,
Removing it first for fear that Priam might see his son
And in his grief be unable to control his anger 630
At the sight of his child, and that this would arouse
Achilles' passion and he would kill the old man
And so sin against the commandments of Zeus.

After the female slaves had bathed Hector's body
And anointed it with olive, they wrapped it 'round 635
With a beautiful robe and tunic, and Achilles himself
Lifted him up and placed him on a pallet
And with his friends raised it onto the polished cart.
Then he groaned and called out to Patroclus:

"Don't be angry with me, dear friend, if somehow 640
You find out, even in Hades, that I have released
Hector to his father. He paid a handsome price,
And I will share it with you, as much as is right."

Achilles reentered his hut and sat down again
In his ornately decorated chair 645
Across the room from Priam, and said to him:

"Your son is released, sir, as you ordered.
He is lying on a pallet. At dawn's first light
You will go see him yourself.
    Now let's think about supper. 650
Even Niobe remembered to eat
Although her twelve children were dead in her house,

Six daughters and six sturdy sons.
Apollo killed them with his silver bow,
And Artemis, showering arrows, angry with Niobe                    655
Because she compared herself to beautiful Leto.
Leto, she said, had borne only two, while she
Had borne many. Well, these two killed them all.
Nine days they lay in their gore, with no one
To bury them, because Zeus had turned                            660
The people to stone. On the tenth day
The gods buried them. But Niobe remembered
She had to eat, exhausted from weeping.
Now she is one of the rocks in the lonely hills
Somewhere in Sipylos, a place they say is haunted                 665
By nymphs who dance on the Achelous' banks,
And although she is stone she broods on the sorrows
The gods gave her.
                    Well, so should we, old sir,
Remember to eat. You can mourn your son later                    670
When you bring him to Troy. You owe him many tears."


A moment later Achilles was up and had slain
A silvery sheep. His companions flayed it
And prepared it for a meal, sliced it, spitted it,
Roasted the morsels and drew them off the spits.                 675
Automedon set out bread in exquisite baskets
While Achilles served the meat. They helped themselves
And satisfied their desire for food and drink.
Then Priam, son of Dardanus, gazed for a while
At Achilles, so big, so much like one of the gods,               680
And Achilles returned his gaze, admiring
Priam's face, his words echoing in his mind.


When they had their fill of gazing at each other,
Priam, old and godlike, broke the silence:


"Show me to my bed now, prince, and quickly,                     685
So that at long last I can have the pleasure of sleep.
My eyes have not closed since my son lost his life
Under your hands. I have done nothing but groan

And brood over my countless sorrows,
Rolling in the dung of my courtyard stables.                    *690*
Finally I have tasted food and let flaming wine

Pass down my throat. I had eaten nothing till now."
Achilles ordered his companions and women
To set bedsteads on the porch and pad them
With fine, dyed rugs, spread blankets on top,                    *695*
And cover them over with fleecy cloaks.
The women went out with torches in their hands
And quickly made up two beds. And Achilles,
The great sprinter, said in a bitter tone:

"You will have to sleep outside, dear Priam.                     *700*
One of the Achaean counselors may come in,
As they always do, to sit and talk with me,
As well they should. If one of them saw you here
In the dead of night, he would tell Agamemnon,
And that would delay releasing the body.                        *705*
But tell me this, as precisely as you can.
How many days do you need for the funeral?
I will wait that long and hold back the army."

And the old man, godlike Priam, answered:

"If you really want me to bury my Hector,                        *710*
Then you could do this for me, Achilles.
You know how we are penned in the city,
Far from any timber, and the Trojans are afraid.
We would mourn him for nine days in our halls,
And bury him on the tenth, and feast the people.                *715*
On the eleventh we would heap a barrow over him,
And on the twelfth day fight, if fight we must."

And Achilles, strong, swift, and godlike:

"You will have your armistice."

And he clasped the old man's wrist                               *720*
So he would not be afraid.
                    And so they slept,

Priam and his herald, in the covered courtyard,
Each with a wealth of thoughts in his breast.
But Achilles slept inside his well-built hut,                    725
And by his side lay lovely Briseis.
Gods and heroes slept the night through,
Wrapped in soft slumber. Only Hermes
Lay awake in the dark, pondering how
To spirit King Priam away from the ships                         730
And elude the strong watchmen at the camp's gates.
He hovered above Priam's head and spoke:

"Well, old man, you seem to think it's safe
To sleep on and on in the enemy camp
Since Achilles spared you. Think what it cost you              735
To ransom your son. Your own life will cost
Three times that much to the sons you have left
If Agamemnon and the Greeks know you are here."

Suddenly the old man was afraid. He woke up the herald.
Hermes harnessed the horses and mules                         740
And drove them through the camp. No one noticed.
And when they reached the ford of the Xanthus,
The beautiful, swirling river that Zeus begot,
Hermes left for the long peaks of Olympus.

D awn spread her saffron light over earth,                     745
And they drove the horses into the city
With great lamentation. The mules pulled the corpse.

No one in Troy, man or woman, saw them before
Cassandra, who stood like golden Aphrodite
On Pergamum's height. Looking out she saw                     750
Her dear father standing in the chariot
With the herald, and then she saw Hector
Lying on the stretcher in the mule cart.
And her cry went out through all the city:

"Come look upon Hector, Trojan men and women,                 755
If ever you rejoiced when he came home alive
From battle, a joy to the city and all its people."

She spoke. And there was not a man or woman
Left in the city, for an unbearable sorrow
Had come upon them. They met Priam by the gates 760
As he brought the body through, and in the front
Hector's dear wife and queenly mother threw themselves
On the rolling cart and pulled out their hair
As they clasped his head amid the grieving crowd.
They would have mourned Hector outside the gates 765
All the long day until the sun went down,
Had not the old man spoken from his chariot:

"Let the mules come through. Later you will have
Your fill of grieving, after I have brought him home."

He spoke, and the crowd made way for the cart. 770
And they brought him home and laid him
On a corded bed, and set around him singers
To lead the dirge and chant the death song.
They chanted the dirge, and the women with them.
White-armed Andromache led the lamentation 775
As she cradled the head of her man-slaying Hector:

"You have died young, husband, and left me
A widow in the halls. Our son is still an infant,
Doomed when we bore him. I do not think
He will ever reach manhood. No, this city 780
Will topple and fall first. You were its savior,
And now you are lost. All the solemn wives
And children you guarded will go off soon
In the hollow ships, and I will go with them.
And you, my son, you will either come with me 785
And do menial labor for a cruel master,
Or some Greek will lead you by the hand
And throw you from the tower, a hideous death,
Angry because Hector killed his brother,
Or his father, or son. Many, many Greeks 790
Fell in battle under Hector's hands.
Your father was never gentle in combat.
And so all the townspeople mourn for him,

And you have caused your parents unspeakable
Sorrow, Hector, and left me endless pain.                        *795*
You did not stretch your hand out to me
As you lay dying in bed, nor did you whisper
A final word I could remember as I weep
All the days and nights of my life."

The women's moans washed over her lament,                        *800*
And from the sobbing came Hecuba's voice:

"Hector, my heart, dearest of all my children,
The gods loved you when you were alive for me,
And they have cared for you also in death.
My other children Achilles sold as slaves                        *805*
When he captured them, shipped them overseas
To Samos, Imbros, and barren Lemnos.
After he took your life with tapered bronze
He dragged you around Patroclus' tomb, his friend
Whom you killed, but still could not bring him back.             *810*
And now you lie here for me as fresh as dew,
Although you have been slain, like one whom Apollo
Has killed softly with his silver arrows."

The third woman to lament was Helen.

"Oh, Hector, you were the dearest to me by far                   *815*
Of all my husband's brothers. Yes, Paris
Is my husband, the godlike prince
Who led me to Troy. I should have died first.
This is now the twentieth year
Since I went away and left my home,                              *820*
And I have never had an unkind word from you.
If anyone in the house ever taunted me,
Any of my husband's brothers or sisters,
Or his mother—my father-in-law was kind always—
You would draw them aside and calm them                         *825*
With your gentle heart and gentle words.
And so I weep for you and for myself,
And my heart is heavy, because there is no one left

In all wide Troy who will pity me
Or be my friend. Everyone shudders at me."                    *830*

And the people's moan came in over her voice.

Then the old man, Priam, spoke to his people:

"Men of Troy, start bringing wood to the city,
And have no fear of an Argive ambush.
When Achilles sent me from the black ships,                    *835*
He gave his word he would not trouble us
Until the twelfth day should dawn."

He spoke, and they yoked oxen and mules
To wagons, and gathered outside the city.
For nine days they hauled in loads of timber.                    *840*
When the tenth dawn showed her mortal light,
They brought out their brave Hector
And all in tears lifted the body high
Onto the bier, and threw on the fire.

Light blossomed like roses in the eastern sky.                    *845*

The people gathered around Hector's pyre,
And when all of Troy was assembled there
They drowned the last flames with glinting wine.
Hector's brothers and friends collected
His white bones, their cheeks flowered with tears.                    *850*
They wrapped the bones in soft purple robes
And placed them in a golden casket, and laid it
In the hollow of the grave, and heaped above it
A mantle of stones. They built the tomb
Quickly, with lookouts posted all around                    *855*
In case the Greeks should attack early.
When the tomb was built, they all returned
To the city and assembled for a glorious feast
In the house of Priam, Zeus' cherished king.

That was the funeral of Hector, breaker of horses.                    *860*

# Major Characters

## Gods and Goddesses

**Aphrodite** (Af-ro-deye´-tee): Goddess of love and beauty. Daughter of Zeus and Dione in the *Iliad*. Aphrodite is pro-Trojan, due in part to her affinity for Paris Alexander, who in other versions awarded her the prize of the Golden Apple for being the most beautiful of the goddesses.

**Apollo** (A-pol´-oh): Patron god of many areas, including music and the arts. Son of Zeus and Leto; brother of Artemis. Also known as Phoebus Apollo, Lord of the Silver Bow, and the Far-Shooter (for his role in bringing death by natural causes to men). Apollo is pro-Trojan in the *Iliad*.

**Ares** (Ai´-reez): God of war. Son of Zeus and Hera. Ares is pro-Trojan in the *Iliad*, although at times he appears as an impartial representative of bloodshed and the cruelties of war.

**Artemis** (Ar´-te-mis): Goddess of the hunt and the moon. Daughter of Zeus and Leto; sister of Apollo. Like her brother, Artemis brings natural death to mortals, although she is the slaughterer of female mortals in particular. She is pro-Trojan in the *Iliad*.

**Athena** (A-thee´-na): Goddess of wisdom, crafts, and battle. Daughter of Zeus, usually said to have sprung from his head. Also called Pallas Athena. Athena is powerfully pro-Achaean in the *Iliad* and has particular favorite heroes on that side.

**Charis** (Ka´-ris): One of the Graces, goddesses of beauty and grace. Wife of Hephaestus in the *Iliad*.

**Cronion** (Kro´-nee-on): Son of Cronus. See Zeus.

**Dione** (Deye-oh´-nee): A goddess of the early generation, either a Titan or an Oceanid. Mother of Aphrodite in the *Iliad*.

**Eris** (Er´-is): Goddess of Discord and Strife.

**Hades** (Hay-deez): God of the Underworld, sometimes synonymous with death. Son of Cronus and Rhea; brother of Zeus, Poseidon, and Hera;

husband of Persephone. Hades shows no partiality to the Achaeans or the Trojans.

**Hebe** (Hee´-bee): Goddess of youth and beauty. Daughter of Zeus and Hera. She serves as a palace helper to the gods on Olympus.

**Hephaestus** (He-feyes´-tus): God of fire and patron of metalworkers. Son of Zeus and Hera; husband of Charis in the *Iliad*. Hephaestus is pro-Achaean, although his major roles are to make peace between his parents and to create magically endowed objects, in particular Achilles' armor.

**Hera** (Hee´-ra): Queen of the Olympian gods. Daughter of Cronus and Rhea; wife of Zeus; mother of Ares, Hephaestus, and Hebe. Hera is powerfully pro-Achaean in the *Iliad*, to the extent that she is at war with her husband.

**Hermes** (Hur´-meez): God who serves as messenger for the Olympians. Son of Zeus and Maia. Hermes is technically pro-Achaean, but has a larger role as a messenger and guide, including guiding Priam, the Trojan king, to the Achaean camp.

**Iris** (Eye´-ris): Goddess of the rainbow and a messenger for the Olympians. Daughter of the Titan Thaumas and the Oceanid Electra.

**Leto** (Lee´-toh): A Titan goddess. Daughter of Coeus and Phoebe; mother of the twins Apollo and Artemis, sired by Zeus. Leto is pro-Trojan, given that her beloved children are strong allies of the Trojans.

**Poseidon** (Po-seye´-don): God of the sea. Son of Cronus and Rhea; brother of Zeus, Hades, and Hera. In the *Iliad*, Poseidon is generally pro-Achaean, although at times he favors certain Trojans.

**Themis** (The´-mis): Titan goddess of law and order. Daughter of Uranus and Gaia.

**Thetis** (The´-tis): A sea goddess, one of the Nereids. Daughter of Nereus and Doris; wife of Peleus; mother of Achilles. Thetis' main concern in the *Iliad* is watching out for her mighty son and securing his desires.

**Xanthus** (Xan´-thus): 1. God of the river near Troy, called by men Scamander. In the battle of the gods, Xanthus fittingly takes his place on the Trojan side. 2. One of Achilles' two immortal horses (Balius is the other).

**Zeus** (Zyoos): The supreme god of Olympus, known as the father of gods and men. Son of Cronus and Rhea; husband of Hera; father of Athena,

Aphrodite, Ares, Apollo, Artemis, Hephaestus, and others. Zeus' position in the *Iliad* is generally impartial except when he is influenced by special requests.

## The Greeks (Achaeans, Argives, and Danaans)

**Achilles** (A-kil´-eez): Son of Peleus, King of Phthia, and Thetis, a sea goddess. Leader of the Myrmidons, the contingent from Phthia, and their fifty ships. Central character whose actions determine the course of the epic.

**Agamemnon** (Ag-a-mem´-non): Son of Atreus and Aerope; brother of Menelaus; husband of Clytemnestra. Commander in chief of the Greek forces and leader of the contingent from Argos and Mycenae and their hundred ships. His quarrel with Achilles sets the plot in motion.

**Ajax** (Ay´-jax) (1): Son of Telamon and Periboea; half-brother of Teucer. Leader of the contingent from Salamis and their twelve ships. Also called Great Ajax and Telamonian Ajax. Since he is known as the greatest in battle next to Achilles, his ships guard the flank opposite that guarded by Achilles. To be distinguished from the lesser Ajax (2).

**Ajax** (2): Son of Oïleus and Eriopis. Leader of the contingent from Locris and their forty ships. He is called Little Ajax, Oïlean Ajax, or Locrian Ajax to distinguish him from Great Ajax (1).

**Antilochus** (An-ti´-lo-kus): Son of Nestor and Eurydice or Anaxibia. Brother of Thrasymedes and co-leader with him and their father of the contingent from Pylos and its ninety ships. Antilochus contributes significantly in combat throughout the epic.

**Automedon** (Aw-to´-me-don): Son of Diores. Charioteer of Achilles' immortal horses.

**Calchas** (Kal´-kas): Son of Thestor. The foremost Greek seer, consulted by the Greeks at key moments of the expedition to Troy.

**Diomedes** (Deye-o-mee´-deez): Son of Tydeus and Deïpyle. Leader with Sthenelus of the contingent from Argos and Tiryns and their eighty ships. Known as one of the greatest Greek fighters and sometimes paired with Odysseus in exploits.

**Epeius** (E-pee´-us): Son of Panopeus. A Phocian fighter who participates in the funeral games as a boxing champion and is known elsewhere as the builder of the Trojan Horse, the war machine that eventually conquers Troy.

**Eumelus** (Yoo-mee´-lus): Son of Admetus and Alcestis. Leader of the Thessalian contingent from Pherae and their eleven ships. Known for his famous horses, he participates in the funeral games as a charioteer.

**Euryalus** (Yoo-reye´-a-lus): Son of Mecisteus. One of the leaders of the contingent from Argos under Diomedes. He participates in the funeral games as a boxer.

**Eurybates** (Yoo-ri´-ba-teez): A principal herald or official messenger of Agamemnon and the Greek forces; his name means "wide walker."

**Eurypylus** (Yoo-ri´-pi-lus): Son of Euaemon and Opis. Leader of one of the Thessalian contingents, with forty ships.

**Helen** (He´-len): Daughter of Zeus and Leda. Originally the wife of Menelaus of Sparta; in the *Iliad*, wife of Paris of Troy. According to ancient mythology, she was the most beautiful woman in the world. In spite of her married status, she was offered as a bride to Paris Alexander by the goddess Aphrodite, on the condition that he would award the Golden Apple of Discord to her. Helen then became known as the cause of the Trojan war, although other reasons for the war are mentioned in Homer and other versions of Helen's story exist in other sources.

**Idomeneus** (Eye-do´-men-yoos): Son of Deucalion. Leader of the contingent from the island of Crete and its eighty ships. One of the most prominent Greek fighters, although older than most.

**Leitus** (Lee´-i-tus): Son of Alectryon and Cleobule. Co-leader with Peneleos of the Boeotian contingent and its fifty ships.

**Leonteus** (Le-on´-tyoos): Son of Coronus. Co-leader with Polypoetes of the Lapith contingent and its forty ships. The two are instrumental in repelling the Trojans' attack on the ships.

**Machaon** (Ma-kay´-on): Son of Asclepius. Co-leader with his brother Podalirius of the Thessalian contingent from Tricca and Oechalia and its thirty ships. A Greek warrior best known, like his brother, for medical skills inherited from his famous father.

**Meges** (Me´-jeez): Son of Phyleus and Ctimene. Leader of the contingent from Dulichium and its forty ships.

**Meleager** (Me-lee-ay´-ger): Son of Oeneus and prince of Calydon. Out of pride, he refuses to defend his people until too late.

**Menelaus** (Me-ne-lay´-us): Son of Atreus and Aerope; brother of Agamemnon, the commander in chief; husband of Helen, who was taken from his home by Paris. Leader of the Lacedaemonian contingent from the Peloponnese and its sixty ships. A prominent Greek warrior.

**Menestheus** (Me-nes´-thyoos): Son of Peteos. Leader of the Athenian contingent and its fifty ships.

**Meriones** (Me-reye´-o-neez): Son of Molus. Second in command under Idomeneus of the contingent from Crete and its eighty ships. A leading Greek warrior and a major participant in the funeral games.

**Myrmidons** (Mir´-mi-dons): Achilles' men from Phthia in northwest Greece.

**Nestor** (Nes´-tor): Son of Neleus and Chloris. Leader with his two sons, Antilochus and Thrasymedes, of the contingent from Pylos and its ninety ships. Although known principally as a wise counsellor to the Greeks and as the oldest among their warriors, Nestor still participates in battle to some degree.

**Odysseus** (O-dis´-yoos): Son of Laertes and Anticleia. Leader of the contingent from the island of Ithaca and its twelve ships. Odysseus serves as a prominent fighter, orator, and general troubleshooter for the Greeks. He is the hero of Homer's *Odyssey*, which tells of his return home.

**Patroclus** (Pa-tro´-klus): Son of Menoetius. Greek warrior with the Myrmidon contingent and best friend of Achilles, its leader. Patroclus is a key figure in the *Iliad* because of his decision to fight in Achilles' place.

**Peleus** (Pee´-lee-us): King of Phthia and father of Achilles.

**Peneleos** (Pee-ne´-lee-ohs): Son of Hippalcimus and Asterope. Co-leader with Leitus of the Boeotian contingent and its fifty ships.

**Phoenix** (Fee´-nix): Son of Amyntor. Greek warrior with the Myrmidons and friend and mentor of Achilles, whose father Peleus made Phoenix king of the Dolopians.

**Podalirius** (Po-da-leye´-ri-us): Son of Asclepius and Epione. Co-leader with his brother Machaon of the Thessalian contingent from Tricca and Oechalia and its thirty ships. A Greek warrior best known, along with his brother, for medical skills inherited from his famous father.

**Polypoetes** (Po-li-pee´-teez): Son of Peirithous and Hippodameia. Co-leader with Leonteus of the Lapith contingent and its forty ships. The two are instrumental in repelling the Trojans' attack on the ships.

**Sthenelus** (Sthen´-e-lus): Son of Capaneus and Evadne. A close friend of Diomedes and second in command under him of the contingent from Argos and its eighty ships.

**Talthybius** (Tal-thi´-bi-us): The principal herald, or official messenger, for Agamemnon and the Greek forces.

**Telamonian Ajax** (Te-le-mo´-ni-an): See Ajax 1.

**Teucer** (Tyoo´-sur): Son of Telamon and Hesione. The illegitimate half-brother of Telamonian (or Great) Ajax, he accompanies the contingent from Salamis and is a notable Greek warrior, particularly with the bow.

**Thersites** (Thur-seye´-teez): Son of Agrius. A Greek warrior known for raucous and rebellious speeches in assemblies.

**Thrasymedes** (Thra-si-mee´-deez): Son of Nestor and Eurydice or Anaxibia. Brother of Antilochus and co-leader with him and their father of the contingent from Pylos. He was known as chief among the sentinels.

**Tlepolemus** (Tle-po´-le-mus): Son of the great hero Heracles and Astyocheia. Leader of the contingent from Rhodes and its nine ships.

## The Trojans (Dardanians) and Allies

**Aeneas** (Ee-nee´-as): Son of Anchises and the goddess Aphrodite. A Trojan fighter of repute who would survive to establish the ruling line of Rome.

**Agenor** (A-je´-nor): Son of Antenor and one of Troy's leading heroes.

**Andromache** (An-dro´-ma-kee): Daughter of Eëtion; wife of Hector; mother of Scamandrius, who was also called Astyanax ("city lord") for his father's glory. She lost her birth family to Achilles earlier in the war and fears losing her husband and child as well.

**Antenor** (An-tee´-nor): Wise Trojan counsellor. Husband of the priestess of Athena, Theano, and father of many sons killed by the Achaeans.

**Astyanax** (A-steye´-a-nax): Infant son of the Trojan hero Hector and his wife Andromache. His given name is Scamandrius, but he is called Astyanax ("city lord") to honor his father. The child is the most likely heir to the Trojan realm and the subject of much concern on the part of his parents.

**Briseis** (Breye-see´-is): Daughter of Briseus. A war prize awarded to Achilles after he sacked Lyrnessus, she was subsequently taken away by Agamemnon.

**Cassandra** (Ka-san´-dra): Daughter of King Priam and Hecuba; sister of Hector, Paris, Helenus, and Deïphobus. Known elsewhere for her prophetic abilities and as an oracle who is never believed.

**Cebriones** (Se-breye´-o-neez): Illegitimate son of King Priam. Warrior and charioteer of his half-brother Hector.

**Chryseis** (Kreye-see´-is): Daughter of Chryses. War prize awarded to Agamemnon as his share of the looting and subsequently ransomed by her father.

**Chryses** (Kreye´-seez): Priest of Apollo who comes to the Achaean camp to ransom his daughter Chryseis, war prize of Agamemnon.

**Deïphobus** (Dee-i´-fo-bus): Son of King Priam and Hecuba; brother of Hector, Paris, Helenus, and Cassandra. Trojan warrior who consults with Hector on strategy.

**Dolon** (Doh´-lon): Son of Eumedes. A Trojan sent to spy on the Achaean forces, he runs into the enemy with disastrous consequences.

**Euphorbus** (Yoo-for´-bus): Son of Panthous and Phrontis. Trojan warrior who wounds Patroclus.

**Glaucus** (Glaw´-kus): Son of Hippolochus. Co-leader with his cousin Sarpedon of the Lycians, Trojan allies. Glaucus is notable as well for his descent from Bellerophon, one of the great heroes of Greek mythology, who in other mythological versions performed glorious feats on the back of the winged horse Pegasus.

**Hector** (Hek´-tor): Oldest son of King Priam and Hecuba; brother of Paris, Helenus, Deïphobus, and Cassandra; husband of Andromache. Leader of the Trojans in battle and their foremost fighter; known as the defense of the city of Troy.

**Hecuba** (He´-kew-ba): Daughter of Dymas, King of Phrygia, and Eunoe. Official consort of King Priam of Troy and mother of many of his children, including Hector, Paris, Helenus, Deïphobus, Cassandra, and Laodice. Known as a prototype of the grieving mother who must face tragic losses in war.

**Helenus** (He´-le-nus): Son of King Priam and Hecuba; brother of Hector, Paris, Deïphobus, and Cassandra. A Trojan fighter and seer, he was awarded the gift of prophecy by Apollo. In other mythological versions, he is said to have become dissatisfied with the Trojans for various reasons and to have gone over to the Achaean side, helping them by means of his prophetic knowledge.

**Idaeus** (Eye-dee´-us): The principal herald, or official messenger, of King Priam and the Trojan forces.

**Laodice** (Lay-o´-di-see): Daughter of King Priam and Hecuba. Sometimes called the most beautiful of their daughters.

**Lycians** (Li´-shunz): People on the southern coast of Asia Minor, allies of the Trojans. Sarpedon is their commander.

**Pandarus** (Pan´-da-rus): Son of King Lycaon of Lycia. Leader of the Troes and a bowman whose role in the *Iliad* is limited mainly to that of peace-breaker. In later mythology Pandarus' role is expanded considerably, although it generally involves the aspect of treachery.

**Paris** (Pa´-ris): Son of King Priam and Hecuba; brother of Hector, Helenus, Deïphobus, and Cassandra. Also called Alexander. A leading Trojan fighter, Paris is better known as the cause of the Trojan war through his seduction of Helen, wife of Menelaus of Sparta.

**Polydamas** (Po-li´-da-mas): Son of Panthous and Phrontis. A Trojan fighter who sometimes advises Hector on strategy.

**Priam** (Preye´-am): Son of Laomedon; husband of Hecuba; father of Hector, Paris, Helenus, Deïphobus, Cassandra, Laodice, and many others. The wealthy and aged ruler of Troy.

**Rhesus** (Ree´-sus): Son of Eïoneus. A Thracian king and ally of the Trojans who arrives late in the war with his famous snow-white horses to do battle with the Achaeans.

**Sarpedon** (Sar-pee´-don): Son of Zeus and Laodamia. Co-leader with his cousin Glaucus of the Lycians, allies of the Trojans.

**Theano** (Thee-ay´-no): Daughter of Cisseus, a king of Thrace; wife of Antenor and mother of his many sons. Priestess of Athena at Troy.

# Suggestions for Further Reading

*Homeri Opera*. Ed. D. B. Monro and T. W. Allen. Vols. I and II. Oxford
  Classical Texts. London, 1920.

*The Iliad: A Commentary*. General Ed., G. S. Kirk. Vol. I: Books 1–4, Kirk.
  Cambridge, England, 1985. Vol. II: Books 5–8, Kirk, 1990. Vol. III:
  Books 9–12, J. B. Hainsworth; Vol. IV: Books 13–16, Richard Janko;
  Vol. V: Books 17–20, Mark W. Edwards; Vol. VI: Books 21–24, Nicholas
  Richardson.


Arnold, Matthew. "On Translating Homer." In *On the Classical Tradition*,
  ed. R. H. Super. Michigan University Press. Ann Arbor and London,
  1960.

Austin, Norman. *Archery at the Dark of the Moon: Poetic Problems in Homer's
  Odyssey*. University of California Press. Berkeley, Los Angeles, and Lon-
  don, 1975.

Bespaloff, Rachel. *On the Iliad*. Mary McCarthy, trans. New York, 1947.

Bowra, Sir Maurice. *Tradition and Design in the Iliad*. Greenwood Press.
  London, 1930.

Clarke, Howard. *Homer's Readers: A Historical Introduction to the Iliad and the
  Odyssey*. University of Delaware Press. Newark, Del., 1981.

Edwards, Mark W. *Homer: Poet of the Iliad*. Johns Hopkins University Press.
  Baltimore, Md., and London, 1987.

Griffin, Jasper. *Homer on Life and Death*. Clarendon Press. Oxford, 1980.

Kirk, G. S. *The Songs of Homer*. Cambridge University Press. Cambridge,
  England, 1962.

Lamberton, R., and J. J. Keaney, eds. *Homer's Ancient Readers: The
  Hermeneutics of Greek Epic's Earliest Exegetes*. Princeton University
  Press. Princeton, N.J., 1992.

Lord, Albert. *The Singer of Tales*. Harvard University Press. Cambridge,
  Mass., 1960.

Lord, Albert. *The Singer Resumes the Tale*. M. L. Lord, ed. Cornell Univer-
  sity Press. Ithaca, N.Y., 1995.

Martin, Richard. *The Language of Heroes: Speech and Performance in the Iliad*.
  Cornell University Press. Ithaca, N.Y., 1989.

Moulton, Carroll. *Similes in the Homeric Poems.* Vandenhoeck und Ruprecht. Göttingen, Germany, 1977.

Mueller, Martin. *The Iliad.* Allen & Unwin. London, 1984.

Nagler, Michael. *Spontaneity and Tradition: A Study in the Oral Art of Homer.* University of California Press. Berkeley, Los Angeles, and London, 1974.

Nagy, Gregory. *The Best of the Achaeans: Concepts of the Hero in Archaic Greek Poetry.* Johns Hopkins University Press. Baltimore, Md., and London, 1979.

Owen, E. T. *The Story of the Iliad.* Reprint Bolchazy-Carducci. Wauconda, Ill., 1989.

Page, Sir Denys. *History and the Homeric Iliad.* Sather Classical Lectures, vol. 31. University of California Press. Berkeley, Los Angeles, and London, 1959.

Parry, Milman. *The Making of Homeric Verse: The Collected Papers of Milman Parry.* Adam Parry, ed. Clarendon Press. Oxford, 1971.

Powell, Barry, and Ian Morris, eds. *A New Companion to Homer.* Brill. Leiden, 1996.

Redfield, J. M. *Nature and Culture in the Iliad: The Tragedy of Hector.* University of Chicago Press. Chicago and London, 1975. Expanded edition: Duke University Press. Durham, N.C., and London, 1994.

Rutherford, R. B. *Homer.* Greece and Rome. New surveys in the classics, no. 26. Oxford University Press, 1966.

Schein, Seth L. *The Mortal Hero: An Introduction to Homer's Iliad.* University of California Press. Berkeley, Los Angeles, and London, 1984.

Segal, Charles. *The Theme of the Mutilation of the Corpse in the Iliad.* Mnemosyne, supp. vol. 17. Leiden, The Netherlands, 1971.

Shay, Jonathan. *Achilles in Vietnam: Combat Trauma and the Undoing of Character.* Athenaeum. New York, 1994.

Shive, David M. *Naming Achilles.* Oxford University Press. New York, 1987.

Silk, M. S. *Homer: The Iliad.* Cambridge University Press. Cambridge, England, 1987.

Slatkin, Laura M. *The Power of Thetis: Allusion and Interpretation in the Iliad.* University of California Press. Berkeley, Los Angeles, and London, 1991.

Steiner, George, and Robert Fagles, eds. *Homer: A Collection of Critical Essays.* Maynard Mack, ed. Twentieth Century Views. Englewood Cliffs, N.J., 1962.

Taplin, Oliver. *Homeric Soundings: The Shaping of the Iliad.* Oxford University Press. New York and London, 1995.

Vivante, Paolo. *Homer.* John Herington, ed. Hermes Books. Yale University Press. New Haven and London, 1985.

Wace, Alan J. B., and Frank Stubbings. *A Companion to Homer.* Macmillan. London, 1962.

Wade-Gery, H. T. *The Poet of the Iliad.* Cambridge, England, 1952.

Weil, Simone. *The Iliad or The Poem of Force.* Mary McCarthy, trans. Politics Pamphlet No. 1. New York, n.d. Reprint. Wallingford, Penn., n.d.

Whitman, Cedric H. *Homer and the Heroic Tradition.* Harvard University Press. Cambridge, Mass., and London, 1958.

Wright, John. *Essays on the Iliad: Selected Modern Criticism.* Indiana University Press. Bloomington, 1978.